ANITA SARKEESIAN & EBONY ADAMS

# HISTORY VS WOMEN

THE **DEFIANT LIVES** THAT
THEY **DON'T WANT** YOU TO **KNOW**

WITH ILLUSTRATIONS BY T. S. ABE

FEIWEL AND FRIENDS
NEW YORK

A FEIWEL AND FRIENDS BOOK

An imprint of Macmillan Publishing Group, LLC

175 Fifth Avenue, New York, NY 10010

Our books may be purchased in bulk for promotional, educational, or business use.

Please contact your local bookseller or the Macmillan Corporate and Premium Sales Department

at (800) 221-7945 ext. 5442 or by e-mail at MacmillanSpecialMarkets@macmillan.com.

Library of Congress Cataloging-in-Publication Data

Names: Sarkeesian, Anita, author. | Adams, Ebony, author.

Title: History vs women : the defiant lives that they don't want you to know /

Anita Sarkeesian and Ebony Adams, PhD.

Other titles: History versus women

Description: First Edition. | New York : Feiwel and Friends, [2018] |

Audience: Age: 14–18. | Includes bibliographical references.

Identifiers: LCCN 2018002811 (print) | LCCN 2018012728 (ebook) |

ISBN 9781250146724 (E-book) | ISBN 9781250146731 (hardcover)

Subjects: LCSH: Women—History—Juvenile literature. |

Feminism—Juvenile literature. | Culture—Juvenile literature.

Classification: LCC HQ1121 (ebook) | LCC HQ1121 .S27 2018 (print) | DDC 305.42—dc23

LC record available at https://lccn.loc.gov/2018002811

Book design by April Ward and Sammy Yuen

Feiwel and Friends logo designed by Filomena Tuosto

First edition, 2018

1  3  5  7  9  10  8  6  4  2

fiercereads.com

# TABLE OF CONTENTS

TO ALL THE WOMEN WHOSE STORIES

WERE NEVER TOLD, WHOSE SONGS

WERE NEVER SUNG, AND WHOSE

WORKS WERE NEVER CELEBRATED.

MAY THE KNOWLEDGE OF YOUR LIVES

STIR UP AMBITIOUS DREAMS IN NEW

GENERATIONS OF WOMEN WHO WILL

NEVER BE FORGOTTEN.

# BY THEIR WORKS YOU SHALL KNOW THEM

Who cares about a bunch of dead women?

Well, we do, and we think you might, too.

W e're finding it quite tiring that rather than being celebrated as heroes, leaders, and innovators, women are often depicted—and treated—as secondary characters in history. They may be love interests, damsels in distress, sassy best friends, mothers, mistresses, or martyrs—but they rarely exist as anything except footnotes to the stories of the men whose lives and achievements we're told actually matter.

But a closer look at history tells a different story. Did you know the inventor of the novel was a Japanese woman? Or that a Chinese woman ruled a fleet of four hundred pirate ships? Or that a fearless nineteen-year-old in 1930 was the first black woman to make a solo motorcycle ride across America, even though the laws of the time meant she had to sleep outside in gas station parking lots?

# WHEN THEY WERE TOLD THAT WOMEN SHOULD ASPIRE TO BE SUBMISSIVE AND GOOD, THEY DECIDED INSTEAD TO BE DEFIANT AND GREAT.

*History vs Women: The Defiant Lives That They Don't Want You to Know* aims to explore the lives and accomplishments of fascinating women across the world who defied cultural expectations and social pressures that sought to limit their ambition and erase them from the history books. When they were told that women should aspire to be submissive and good, they decided instead to be *defiant* and *great*. Their uncompromising lives and thrilling exploits are a reminder that the stories we tell about women—in TV shows, comic books, and video games, as well as in real life—often reflect the stereotypes and limitations that have been created for them, rather than the world-changing feats they have already achieved, often against incredible odds.

In *History vs Women*, we've gone searching for women across the globe and across generations to draw back the curtain on those phenomenal figures whose stories you may not know, but whose uncompromising lives still reach out to us. Digging deep into the past, we came across scores of forgotten women whose incredible triumphs and historical importance had been lost. It is invigorating and electrifying to reclaim their stories and share them with you. Nevertheless, it's hard not to think about the others: women with inspiring stories of creativity, ambition, perseverance, and brilliance that have been lost forever. The contributions of many women simply weren't valued enough to record. But the greatest tragedy is the sheer number of exceptional minds who never had the opportunity to explore their talents at all because as women, particularly women of color, they were never given an opportunity.

*History vs Women* aims to introduce you to a range of dynamic women across many different races, countries, time periods, and classes. Some of their names might be familiar to you, and we hope you discover new and fascinating parts to their stories. But we suspect that many of the women you'll meet in these pages you'll be hearing about for the first time. We think you'll be as blown away as we are by the colorful tapestries of their lives and the fearsome impact they made on their societies.

The book is divided into five sections:

# RECKLESS REBELS
# REVELATORY SCHOLARS
# RUTHLESS VILLAINS
# RESTLESS ARTISTS
# RELENTLESS AMAZONS

We've deliberately chosen figures across a wide variety of fields, to prove that there's no arena in which women can't make their mark. The "Ruthless Villains" section is especially important to us. It's crucial that we don't simply celebrate the heroic contributions of women in history, but instead recognize that women are fully human and are therefore capable of the heights of heroism . . . or the depths of wickedness. No book about women's history is complete without acknowledging the fullness of women's experiences, and in this book, we certainly don't sugarcoat any gruesome or unsavory history.

Through these captivating stories—and the magnificent artwork that accompanies them—we hope to demonstrate that history is a dynamic, dramatic, *living* thing. To put it simply: If you are like us, and you care about the future of our planet and all the beings on it, you'll want to understand how we got here, to this time, in this moment. To understand the heroes and villains of today, we must understand the heroes and villains of yesterday. So, join us as we initiate you into a secret society of remarkable women. We think you'll like the other members.

# RECKLESS REBELS

Explore the lives of women who teach us that justice
is always worth fighting for, whether on the battlefield,
from the courtroom, or in the press.

L ike the mythical phoenix rising from the ashes, women cannot be destroyed. Keep us out
of school, and we'll learn to read in secret. Tell us we're too weak to compete, and we'll
beat you at your own game. Bar us from the halls of power, and we'll storm the gates and
lift our voices anyway. Despite all that's been done around the world and throughout history
to keep women down, we climb toward the light.

This section is devoted to sharing stories of rebellious women who refused to accept the
status quo. These courageous fighters ignored the direct and indirect calls to say silent, and for
that they sometimes paid a terrible cost. When they wouldn't sit quietly and act "ladylike," they
were met with violent opposition. But despite being despised, feared, and attacked, they kept

# REBELS DON'T GIVE UP. THEY AREN'T AFRAID OF MAKING PEOPLE ANGRY OR GETTING THEIR HANDS DIRTY.

going—even when the odds were stacked against them. From India to Vietnam, from America to Egypt, they challenged powerful people and institutions, regardless of the personal cost.

Being a lightning rod for social change is emotionally taxing and often isolating, but rebels don't give up. They aren't afraid of making people angry or getting their hands dirty. On the battlefield and in the courtroom, they keep marching, speaking up, and fighting for self-determination, religious freedom, and a better world.

For any student of social justice and human rights, the choice about which fearless fighters to include in a work like this presents a tremendous challenge. There are so many women who came before us and paved the way for our activist work today. We only have space to share a small sampling of the breathtaking resilience and courage that women demonstrate every single day. Reckless rebels such as Doria Shafik, one of modern Egypt's pioneering feminists; Ida B. Wells, a crusading black American journalist and anti-lynching campaigner; Mai Bhago, an indomitable Sikh warrior; Lucy Hicks Anderson, a woman at the vanguard of the fight for transgender rights; and Triệu Thị Trinh, one of the mothers of Vietnam, inspire us and give us the courage to fight against police brutality, environmental catastrophe, and discrimination and inhumanity in all their forms. Around the world, women are battling for a just world where all people are treated with dignity and respect. Be inspired by their stories and motivated by their courage, so that one day, we can all be like feminist activist and writer Audre Lorde, who proclaimed that "when I dare to be powerful—to use my strength in the service of my vision, then it becomes less and less important whether I am afraid."[1]

# THIRD CENTURY

# TRIỆU THỊ TRINH

## RIDER ON THE STORM

**R**age into the wind!

Feel the dreadful thunder of mighty war elephants trampling the ground. Raise your fists and sound your terrible war cry.

Survey the indomitable warriors around you, and let the righteous fury of your fight course through your blood.

This is the story of the mighty Bà Triệu (Lady Trieu), third-century freedom fighter from Vietnam and impossible badass.

Born around 225 CE in the mountainous region of northern Vietnam, Triệu Thị Trinh was orphaned at an early age and raised by an elder brother, Triệu Quôc Đạt. While records of her life at this time are difficult to confirm, some accounts speak of an unhappy childhood, suffering under an abusive sister-in-law. Bà Triệu responded to the abuse with the same decisiveness and avenging fury she would wield throughout her short life. The tales say that her spirit cried out at her ill treatment and that she struck a decisive blow for freedom. During one pitched battle, her sister-in-law was killed—deliberately or inadvertently, we will never know. Bà Triệu fled to the haven of the forested mountains.

Deep within those imposing green mountains, she took the first step on the path that would transform her from Triệu Thị Trinh the woman into Bà Triệu the freedom fighter and legend.

For over three hundred years, the Chinese had occupied and ruled Bà Triệu's region of

northern Vietnam with an iron fist. During this period, brutal taxation and exploitation of the poor was commonplace. Expressions of Vietnamese cultural identity, as opposed to the mandated Chinese one, were often ruthlessly suppressed. The desire of wealthy Vietnamese elites for more independence and autonomy was met with varying degrees of resistance—usually harsh.

One of the unsurprising realities of the legend of Bà Triệu is that although her myth is woven throughout Vietnamese histories, her name rarely, if ever, appears in Chinese versions of the same period. There's the understandable and natural impulse to emphasize victories and downplay losses. There's also the cultural effect of Confucianism, as it was interpreted by Chinese leaders of the day. It took for granted that a woman's nature was passive and her social role was to be subservient to men. Imagine how hard it must have been for the Chinese generals warring against fierce females like Bà Triệu to admit defeat at the hands of a woman!

And the Chinese forces did suffer defeat, over and over again. We do not have an overwhelming number of sources, but it is believed that during her martial career, Bà Triệu led more than a thousand men and women into at least thirty decisive battles. Commanding a mighty army, Bà Triệu rebelled against the tyranny of the Chinese and the mandated erasure of Vietnamese ethnic and national identity. In doing so, she became a legend:

Bà Triệu, who towered over men at nine feet tall.

Bà Triệu, who shone in her golden armor and could walk five hundred leagues in a day.

Bà Triệu, whose voice rang out like a temple bell and whose beauty stopped the breath.

Bà Triệu, who could eat bushels of rice in one sitting!

Bà Triệu, who slung her three-foot-long breasts over her shoulders when she rode into battle!

Bà Triệu stands as a larger-than-life figure in the fight for Vietnamese independence and as a woman of the common people. So, Bà Triệu's massive bosom? It was most likely a symbolic thumbing of the nose to later neo-Confucian edicts that demanded women bind their breasts to avoid appearing "indecent" or "unseemly." Think what it means for

Bà Triệu to race across painted canvases or dance through patriotic songs, her colossal bosom proud and defiant. What an image!

But despite Bà Triệu's rousing victories, she was not without detractors at home. Her own brother tried to convince her to live quietly and give up the rebel life, to which she responded:

> I WANT TO RIDE THE STORM, TREAD THE DANGEROUS WAVES, WIN BACK THE FATHERLAND AND DESTROY THE YOKE OF SLAVERY. I DON'T WANT TO BOW DOWN MY HEAD WORKING AS A SIMPLE HOUSEWIFE.[2]

By 248 CE, the Chinese emperor had had enough. He resolved to stamp out the rebellion and Bà Triệu's forces by any means necessary. Bribes flowed, and reinforcements were sent to the front. After several months of fighting, Bà Triệu's army was defeated. Legends say that she chose to commit suicide rather than accept the dishonor of surrender. The Chinese wouldn't finally be driven from Vietnam until 939 CE.

So, what is behind the growth of Bà Triệu from a mere mortal to a literal giant (with three-foot breasts)? Of course these stories are entertaining, but they also highlight something about the way we treat our heroes and, particularly, how we try to make sense of women who succeed in typically male-dominated spheres. It is almost inconceivable to many that an ordinary woman—possessed of great courage, yes, and a strategic mind, but an ordinary woman nonetheless—could inspire devotion from many hundreds of men and lead them to martial victory. So she must have been extraordinary.

It's not hard to see why a figure as dynamic and larger than life as Bà Triệu could capture the imagination of a people. We hold fast to heroes who reflect back to us everything we want to embody. Figures like Robin Hood perform the same function in our Western cultural imagination. Bà Triệu represents an authority-defying, blood-stirring will to fight for the people. In Vietnam, streets are not named after Bà Triệu for her nine-foot height, or her insatiable hunger for rice, but rather for the way she stands tall as a monument to Vietnamese resilience and their will to fight in the face of overwhelming odds.

# MAI BHAGO

## THE HOLY TERROR

**M**ai Bhago was a fearless and dedicated woman, celebrated and remembered within Sikh religious communities, but we suspect she might be as unknown to many of you as she was to us. Western history books too often skip over the stories and defining moments of communities in the global south. And when we do get a peek at the struggles of brown and black folks around the world, patriarchy is there to obscure the contributions of women. Bhago was instrumental in the battle for Sikh religious freedom in the early eighteenth century. Without her commitment to what she believed was right and just, one of the largest religious groups in the world may have been defeated indefinitely.

Mai Bhago was born and raised, along with her brothers, in the village of Jhabal Kalan in the Punjab region of India. Her father taught her both religious devotion and combat skills—skills that Bhago would later use to defend Guru Gobind Singh, the last in the line of "divine spiritual messengers" who founded Sikhism. Sikhs believe one God exists equally for everybody, regardless of gender or race. The religion rejects caste and teaches that one should value truth and compassion and fight for the justice of all people.

During Guru Gobind Singh's time as prophet he encouraged his devotees to be both saints and soldiers. They were to be equally dedicated to resisting oppressive

religious and government forces and to helping the most vulnerable members of society. Guru Gobind Singh stressed the importance of discipline, piety, and reflection in all spiritual matters but was adamant about the righteousness of taking up arms in defense of his people and their beliefs.

Bhago grew up surrounded by this kind of fervor and focus. More than one of her family members served under previous gurus, and Bhago, a skilled warrior, was committed to following in their footsteps.

Bhago and her fellow Sikhs suffered during the long reign of Aurangzeb, the intolerant Mughal emperor. His regime was brutal and unrelenting—unsurprising for a leader who imprisoned his own father and ordered the execution of his eldest brother to consolidate power.

Before Aurangzeb, Mughal emperors had allowed their subjects to follow their own laws and practice their own religion, but Aurangzeb imposed and vigorously enforced Islamic law throughout the conquered lands. Under his reign, Hindu temples were destroyed, and a punitive tax on all non-Muslim subjects was reinstated. Aurangzeb was pitiless in his mission to erase every religion but Islam from his empire, including the Sikhs and Guru Gobind Singh.

But getting to Guru Gobind Singh in

> HER RELENTLESS DETERMINATION WAS SO GALVANIZING THAT SHE EVEN INSPIRED SOME WIVES TO OFFER TO JOIN THE BATTLE THEMSELVES IF THEIR HUSBANDS REFUSED.

1705 meant going through a dedicated but not overwhelming cluster of soldiers who protected him. The small band traveled from hideout to hideout, barely able to survive on the scarce rations they could find. Exhaustion and despair were rampant. Many wanted to give up. Some of them did. In fact, of the fewer than one hundred fighters protecting Guru Gobind Singh, forty of them deserted the cause.

Bhago's fury when she learned of their desertion was frightening to behold. She refused to accept their cowardice. She rode from village to village, rousing the wives and families of the deserters to turn them away. Her relentless determination was so galvanizing that she even inspired some

TO THIS DAY, SIKHS AROUND THE WORLD SHARE THE STORY OF THE WOMAN WHO, THROUGH POWERFUL LEADERSHIP AND SINGLE-MINDED SPIRITUAL DEVOTION, SAVED GURU GOBIND SINGH, AND SIKHISM ITSELF.

wives to offer to join the battle themselves if their husbands refused.

And in the end? All forty deserters returned, this time joined by Mai Bhago herself—and not a moment too soon. After weeks of pursuit, the Mughal army had almost overtaken the guru. The Sikhs were vastly outnumbered, so they had to be especially cunning about their defense. Knowing that the Mughal army was tired and thirsty, Bhago and her men set up close to the only water source for miles around, a reservoir near the village of Khidrana. They cloaked the area in sheets and fabric, which may have been intended to appear from a distance like the assembled camp of a much larger enemy force, or may have been meant to deceive the Mughals into believing that the guru himself was present. When the Mughals approached, the Sikh fighters, hiding in the surrounding area, ambushed them.

When the fighting was over, Mai Bhago stood alone on the field of battle, the only survivor. Her family, her friends, her brethren in the faith—all gone. The Mughals believed that they had carried the day and that Guru Gobind Singh's body lay among the many broken and bleeding dead. Finding the reservoir dry, they shrugged and shuffled off in search of a drink of water.

But Guru Gobind Singh was not dead. Through the valiant efforts of Bhago and her fellow holy warriors, the guru had escaped. He blessed the forty who died as Chali Mukte, the Forty Liberated Ones, and their sacrifice became known as the Battle of Muktsar, meaning "pool of liberation." Bhago recovered from her battle wounds and became one of the guru's personal bodyguards. After his death a few years later, in 1708, Mai Bhago retired and lived to a ripe old age. To this day, Sikhs around the world share the story of the woman who, through powerful leadership and single-minded spiritual devotion, saved Guru Gobind Singh, and Sikhism itself.

# CALL HER BY HER NAME

There is one thing that no one can ever take away from you. That's the knowledge, in your soul, of who you are.

Lucy Hicks Anderson knew who she was. She lived her truth and never wavered, despite the combined weight of the United States legal system, early twentieth-century social mores, and vicious racist attacks pressing in on all sides.

Lucy Hicks Anderson was a black woman born in a body that did not fit who she knew herself to be, and she was arguably the first American to go to court to defend her gender.

In 1886, a beautiful baby was born to the Lawson family in Waddy, Kentucky. While this child was identified at birth as male, from a very young age she knew that she was a girl and insisted on being treated as such. The young girl named herself Lucy and told her family that she would be wearing dresses to school. Confounded, Mrs. Lawson took little Lucy to the local doctor; he advised Lucy's mother to raise her as she would any little girl.

At that point in American history, any kind of understanding or discussion of transgenderism (being born into a body that does not conform to one's gender identity) was sadly lacking. This is not to say that transgender people did not exist before we had the words to describe them—far from it. But

during Lucy's childhood in late nineteenth-century America, it was surprising, and fortunate, that her mother found a medical doctor willing to treat her daughter with the care and dignity that she deserved. Even today, the humanity of too many transgender children is denied because they are surrounded by people who are at best ignorant and at worst hateful and bigoted. Thankfully, Lucy's doctor and mother granted her the opportunity to live as the girl she knew herself to be.

At fifteen, she left school to become a domestic worker. For years she moved from place to place and job to job, working in a Texas hotel for a time and marrying her first husband, Clarence Hicks, in Silver City, New Mexico. She settled in Oxnard, California, a farming town about an hour up the coast from Los Angeles. Her culinary skills opened doors, and she began to cater elaborate parties for Oxnard's rich citizens. She reportedly even won contests for her delectable dinner rolls and fruitcakes. Anderson worked diligently, and the money she saved from her employment as a domestic worker, nanny, and cook allowed her to purchase some property. She bought a brothel—and that's what eventually led to her greatest trouble.

Anderson's brothel was in operation during Prohibition, the period between 1920 and 1933 when alcohol was illegal in America. As a brothel madam, Anderson had already fox-trotted over the lines of propriety, so she served her customers alcohol anyway. She was busted a few times, but she'd built up a great deal of social capital with the notable members of the community (and, we assume, blackmail-worthy information at the brothel), so she was able to escape any aggressive prosecution. Rumor has it that a wealthy banker posted her bail after one arrest so that she could cater his party that evening.

Having divorced Hicks in 1929, Lucy, fifty-eight years old and well established in the Oxnard community, married soldier Reuben Anderson in 1944. But their happiness wasn't to last. A year after they married, a sailor claimed one of the women in Anderson's brothel infected him with venereal disease. All the women had to undergo physical examinations, and a doctor insisted on examining Anderson as well. Her transgender identity was revealed. Sadly, the doctor and the Ventura County prosecutors were not nearly as progressive as Anderson's mother and family doctor back in Kentucky. Lucy was charged with perjury.

In the eyes of the prosecution, Lucy was a man, and she had committed perjury when she signed her marriage license and

# "I DEFY ANY DOCTOR IN THE WORLD TO PROVE THAT I AM NOT A WOMAN. I HAVE LIVED, DRESSED, ACTED JUST WHAT I AM, A WOMAN."

swore that there was no legal objection to the marriage. Only a marriage between a man and a woman was legal at the time. Lucy didn't back down from this fight and stood up for herself. During the trial she argued, "I defy any doctor in the world to prove that I am not a woman," and went on to say, "I have lived, dressed, acted just what I am, a woman."[3] Sadly, she did not win her case. She was convicted, but instead of being sent to prison, she received ten years of probation.

Unfortunately, that wasn't the end of her legal troubles. When Anderson's marriage to her soldier husband was ruled invalid, the US government got involved. First it went after her for failing to register for the draft, as all men between eighteen and forty-five years old were required to do. When her Kentucky birth certificate proved she had been too old to register, she was charged with illegally taking money from the US government as a military wife. Both Lucy and Reuben were convicted of fraud and sentenced to jail time. Lucy was even forbidden, by court order, from wearing women's clothing! After prison, when Anderson tried to return home, she was forcefully barred from living in Oxnard by the local police chief under penalty of prosecution. Anderson moved to Los Angeles, where she quietly lived under the radar until her death in 1954.

Lucy Hicks Anderson didn't position herself at the forefront of the struggle for social justice. She simply wanted to be accepted for who she knew herself to be. She was Lucy. That was all she ever wanted to be, and she was willing to fight for it.

There's something irresistible about underdog stories, where remarkable people rise from humble beginnings to do incredible things against all the odds. But few stories are as dramatic as that of Ida B. Wells, a woman who was born a slave in Mississippi in the midst of the Civil War and became a daring investigative reporter and civil rights crusader. In an era of injustice, she would become the "loudest and most persistent voice for truth."[4]

From an early age, Wells carried exceptional burdens with exceptional courage. She became the head of her household in 1878 at the age of sixteen, when both her parents died suddenly from yellow fever. To support her five brothers and sisters, she set aside her own ambitions for advanced education and started working as a schoolteacher for young children in rural Mississippi.

In 1881, Wells relocated her two younger sisters to Memphis to live with extended family while she searched for better job opportunities and attended Fisk University in Nashville, Tennessee. In 1883, when she was twenty-one years old, Wells boarded a train to Memphis after a visit to Mississippi and seated herself in the first-class ladies car, only to be told that black women were restricted to second class. Not only did she bite the conductor who forcibly tried to remove her, she soon filed a discrimination

lawsuit against the railroad company. She won the initial case, and while it was overturned on appeal, an article she wrote about the experience helped launch her career as a journalist.

In 1892, the course of Wells's life changed forever. Her friend Thomas Moss was murdered by a white mob in Memphis along with two other black men. Their brutal killings inspired Wells, a co-owner and editor of a black newspaper in Memphis, to speak out against the horrors of lynching, an increasingly common tool of terror used against black people in the decades after the Civil War.

Black men were often falsely accused of rape to justify their savage and extrajudicial murders by bloodthirsty mobs, but in a series of widely read articles and pamphlets, Wells argued that lynching had little to do with protecting the honor of women and everything to do with protecting the power of southern white men. Like so many civil rights leaders who would follow in her footsteps—including the civil rights leaders of today—her criticisms were powerful because they took aim not just at the misdeeds of individuals, but at the unexamined institutions of racism and power behind them.

Her groundbreaking analysis changed the national conversation around lynching.

# SHE SAID IT WAS BETTER TO "DIE FIGHTING AGAINST INJUSTICE THAN TO DIE LIKE A DOG OR A RAT IN A TRAP."

Even her future mentor Frederick Douglass called his own writing on the subject "feeble in comparison."[5] Faced with death threats, Wells started carrying a pistol in her purse, but refused to back down from her anti-lynching campaign. She said it was better to "die fighting against injustice than to die like a dog or a rat in a trap."[6]

Wells relocated to New York, where she wrote for papers such as the *New York Age* and began to publish investigative journalism for an even larger audience, including pamphlets that collected statistical documentation of lynching in the South. Her popular anti-lynching speeches eventually took her to Britain, where white audiences seemed far more outraged than many of their American counterparts. Her overseas speaking tour inspired international condemnation of lynching, particularly from British newspapers and politicians, and elevated Wells to the most visible national leader in the anti-lynching movement.

Although Wells often criticized herself for being stubborn and hot tempered, those same qualities made her a fiery orator and a relentless crusader against injustice. Faced with death threats from southern whites and criticisms from moderate black reformers who considered her too radical, Wells refused to compromise her ideals for the sake of comfort, convenience, or even personal safety. After one of her anti-lynching articles "displeased" the white community, an angry mob stormed the office of the paper and destroyed it.

"The way to right wrongs is to turn the light of truth upon them,"[7] proclaimed a broadside advertising one of Wells's lectures. And indeed, Ida B. Wells never failed to shine the light of truth on unspeakable horror, even when it cost her friends and potential allies. Surrounded by hostility and threats from people who wanted to punish her outspokenness because of her race and her gender, she refused to be silenced.

Although she fought for women's rights, Wells was often disappointed by white suffragists who considered racial issues a distraction from the fight against sexism. Some of them even endorsed segregation. During the 1913 women's suffrage parade in Washington, DC, when black women were told to walk at the back, Wells defiantly joined her state's delegation along the parade route. Similarly, she was frustrated by those in the black community who saw women's rights as unimportant to the fight against racism. Caught between the struggles of her race and her gender, Wells often felt like she fought alone.

Wells remained single throughout her twenties despite many suitors and enormous social pressure to marry. In her early thirties, however, she met and fell in love with Ferdinand Barnett, a black Chicago lawyer who was equally passionate about social justice and who wholeheartedly supported her career. They married and had four children, and she continued her work as a reformer until the day she died.

By the time she passed away in 1931 at the age of sixty-eight, Ida B. Wells had profoundly changed the way people looked at race, gender, and violence in America and had transformed herself from a slave who was regarded as property to a woman who, her daughter said, "walked as if she owned the world."[8]

# TWENTIETH CENTURY

## DORIA SHAFIK

## DAUGHTER OF THE NILE

t's impossible to tally the cost to women for standing up and speaking truth to power. The consequences for not being silent are as varied as they are severe. And yet, in all ages and in all places, brave women face isolation, censure, or even death for refusing to back down when powerful men demand that they accept injustice as unchangeable and preordained.

After Egypt gained independence in the early twentieth century, a purposeful drive toward a more "modern" version of the country started to gain steam, increasing capitalist enterprise, expanding literacy— even opening up closed, cloistered architectural styles.

Women were a vital part of this push toward national independence, despite the "harem culture" that had secluded Egyptian women in domestic spaces meant to preserve their modesty and protect men from their potentially damaging influence. Increasing numbers of Egyptian women began to take advantage of freedoms outside the home, like access to higher education, defying the social pressures to remain second-class citizens. At the forefront of this movement was a woman named Doria Shafik.

Doria Shafik was born in 1908 in Tanta, in the Nile delta in northern Egypt. She was the second child of six and a precocious student. As part of Egypt's middle class, Shafik received much of her education in French schools (a relic of France's brief occupation,

which brought French scholars and scientists to the country and led to French becoming the language of the elite). At age sixteen, Shafik distinguished herself as the youngest person in the country to receive a French baccalaureate, and by nineteen, she had won a scholarship to study at the Sorbonne in Paris, one of the world's most rigorous and prestigious universities. While in Paris, she continued to excel academically, earning a doctorate with distinction in 1940. She also married her cousin Nour al-Din Ragai, who was studying law in Paris and with whom she raised two daughters.

After Shafik returned to her native country, she was denied a teaching position at Cairo University, allegedly for being "too modern." What would that have meant? It's entirely likely that after several years of independent living and autonomy in France, Shafik would have chafed at the pervasive restrictions Egyptian women still faced back home. For her thesis, Shafik had written eloquently and persuasively about the ways in which the Koran supported female equality. We can only imagine how the more conservative elements at the university and in society at large saw Shafik. This defining moment in her professional life sparked her visible commitment to improving the station of women in Egypt.

In 1945, Princess Chevikar, first wife of the late King Fu'ād I, offered Shafik the position of editor in chief of *La femme nouvelle*, a literary magazine that bridged Egyptian and Western culture and catered to the tastes of elite Egyptian women who gathered in salons to discuss art and literature. Later that year, Shafik founded her own magazine, *Bint al-Nil* (Daughter of the Nile), which concentrated on women's issues and targeted the broader middle class, with the ambitious goal of educating and empowering all Egyptian women. After the princess died, Shafik took over total control of *La femme nouvelle*, where she furthered opportunities for Egyptian feminists to share their writing and scholarship.

In the following years, Shafik's concern about the condition of women in her country led her to form the Bint al-Nil Union, in the hope that as a unified collective, women could address Egypt's literacy rate, working conditions, and women's lack of agency on the political front.

By 1951, Shafik's activism had started to take on a more active tenor, which proved troubling for Egyptian state officials. Shafik stormed parliament with fifteen hundred other fierce women, from various Egyptian groups, to demand that legislative officials pay heed to the status of women in society.

It was a magnificent sight to behold, and the voices and presence of all those stubborn women must have shaken the assembled men to their core. Sadly, although the parliamentarians issued assurances that they would consider women's rights to vote and sit in parliament, no real, substantive change came from this demonstration. At least, not in the form of immediate changes to Egypt's laws or society.

But there *were* changes, albeit subtle and slow. As Doria Shafik and other mid-twentieth-century feminists like her became more visible in society, they also became more powerful. They helped to normalize the idea that women can, and should, be vocal members of society, with full rights to participate in the decision-making that governed their lives.

In 1952, Shafik successfully lobbied to have Bint al-Nil recognized as an official political party, with herself as president. A few years later, in 1954, Shafik began the eight-day hunger strike that would make her world-famous. Her aim, as always, was to shine a spotlight on Egyptian women's lack of access to the halls of power—in particular, President Muhammad Naguib's recent formation of a constitutional committee with absolutely no women. Shafik only ended her strike once the president issued a statement about forming a constitution that respected the rights of women.

After the successful, stirring conclusion of her hunger strike, Shafik was invited to lecture all over the world, including in the United States, Europe, and Asia. Audiences everywhere were stirred by this woman who lived every day in the belief that we should "never hesitate to act when the feeling of injustice revolts us. To give one's measure with all good faith, the rest will follow as a logical consequence."[9]

In 1956, due to the tireless efforts of Doria Shafik and other fearless feminists, Egyptian women finally achieved a hard-fought battle: the right to vote. It should be noted, however, that women had to apply to vote, demonstrating their literacy; men did not. It was another way in which women have to overcome often unfair obstacles on the road to true equality.

A year after women gained the right to vote, Shafik embarked on a second hunger strike. By this point, Gamal Abdel Nasser had seized the office of the presidency, and Shafik protested what she saw as President Nasser's brutal regime, which suppressed dissent and civic protest. Although she continued to focus on women's rights, this second hunger strike was prompted by her abiding concern with the lack of respect for democratic ideals and devastating blows to human rights she saw in Nasser's militaristic administration.

Unfortunately, President Nasser, though

dictatorial, was quite popular. He responded decisively to Shafik's highly public critique of his power and had her seized from the care of the physicians overseeing her hunger strike. Instead of victory and a worldwide lecture tour, Shafik was sentenced to house arrest, and her name was forbidden to be mentioned in the press. Her magazines were shuttered, and her connection to the public withered.

Friends fled. Colleagues deserted her. She was expelled from Bint al-Nil, the very group she had formed. A coalition of twenty-seven women from different Egyptian women's groups circulated a petition, "Egyptian Women Renounce the Position of Doria Shafik." Where once Shafik had brought many disparate groups together to fight on one accord, now she was considered social and political poison.

It's hard to imagine how difficult this must have been for Shafik. She withdrew into total isolation during her house arrest, only meeting with her family. Even after some of the restrictions were lifted, she remained secluded, having turned to poetry to express the things she could no longer say in public.

Sadly, Doria Shafik took her own life in 1975. She jumped from a balcony, having spent the prior eighteen years cut off from the society and culture she had worked so

## "HERE I AM HEADING TOWARD THE HEIGHTS. . . . ONCE LAUNCHED, YOU MUST NEVER STOP."

hard to improve. At her death, many esteemed writers, thinkers, and activists expressed the inestimable loss her death was for Egyptian society, while taking to task the same society that had abandoned her: "Doria Shafik, this woman, who filled the world with noise and declarations, this woman, upon whom the world's lights were directed wherever she went, this woman, who was the star of Egyptian, Arab, European and American society. People forgot her charge into parliament, demanding the right to vote; they forgot her hunger strike in 1954 for the rights of women and they forgot she lost her freedom and her magazines, her money and her husband because she demanded human rights for the Egyptian people. She paid a horrible price for her resistance when other people gave up. She paid a horrible price for her boldness when all those around her quivered in fear from the sword and the whip."[10]

But as Shafik herself said in one of her poems, "Here I am heading toward the heights. . . . Once launched, you must never stop."[11]

# REVELATORY SCHOLARS

We've all heard about Galileo, Socrates, and Isaac Newton—
but we think it's time you learned about some brilliant women
who would have given them a run for their money.

There's nothing better than sharing stories of women who sat at the head of the class—because no matter what history might suggest, men aren't the only ones with brains.

Trying to trace the history of women's scholarly achievements can be a frustrating endeavor. For instance, we know that women were discoverers, educators, creators, inventors, and philosophers. Yet so many brilliant women, across the world and throughout time, have had to stare down crushing opposition to exercise their natural talents. But despite their astounding drive to succeed, their names—and often their works—have been gradually erased from the historical record and from our collective memories. Retelling and amplifying those stories gives a fuller and more accurate sense of world history.

Frustratingly, many of these women's stories are met with patronizing challenges or outright disbelief. The mind-boggling assumption is that women couldn't possibly have demonstrated

# IT'S HEARTBREAKING TO REFLECT ON ALL THE DAZZLINGLY INTELLECTUAL WOMEN OF THE PAST WHO NEVER HAD THE OPPORTUNITY TO EXPLORE AND SHARE THEIR GIFTS WITH THE WORLD.

such genius. The arguments are pretty ridiculous, but they keep getting recycled, over and over. If a woman is credited with any sort of intelligence, well, then she must have had help from a man. Sometimes critics will imply that her discoveries were obvious and probably didn't require much insight; sometimes they'll just suggest that her work is simply a re-creation of a more brilliant man's work. And it's far from uncommon for scholarly women to find that their achievements are simply stolen wholesale when their male colleagues are given credit.

For these and other reasons, records of learned women from history are often difficult to find and often woefully incomplete.

So what do we know about these forgotten female scholars? One consistent through-line is that it was often women of privilege who had the educational, social, and leisure opportunities to pursue knowledge and invention. Although there were undoubtedly female geniuses from more humble backgrounds, it's almost impossible to find complete records of their lives and work. It's likely that what we know about women like Hypatia, Wang Zhenyi, and Fatima al-Fihri, we know because their privileged social positions allowed some evidence—paltry as it is—of their work to be recorded.

It's heartbreaking to reflect on all the dazzlingly intellectual women of the past who never had the opportunity to explore and share their gifts with the world. Sadly, the situation remains bleak for many women today. Many girls attend poorly funded and segregated schools like those on Chicago's South Side, and many are even prevented from attaining an education because of schools destroyed by war and unrest in places like Iraq and Syria.

Nevertheless, we are hopeful. You've probably heard of Marie Curie, the physicist and chemist who won two Nobel Prizes for her research into radioactivity. Perhaps you have even heard of Ada Lovelace, the

Victorian-era countess whose mathematical genius gave the world the very first computer program, long before the computer as we know it was invented. By introducing you to women you may not know, we hope that you'll be inspired to seek out more inspiring histories and share your own brilliance with the world.

Although the names of these revelatory scholars may be unfamiliar to you, we believe that you will be just as riveted by their stories as we are. You'll learn about a woman in fourth-century Egypt who was such a celebrated mathematical and philosophical mind that students came from miles around to sit at her feet and learn. You'll hear about how just a few centuries later and a couple countries over, a Muslim woman in Morocco founded the world's oldest university. And from our very modern past, we'll tell you about how "human computers"—incredible female mathematicians with rudimentary adding machines—helped send men into space.

THE WOMEN WITHIN THESE PAGES HELPED
BLAZE A TRAIL FOR FUTURE GENERATIONS
OF SCIENTISTS, EDUCATORS, AND LEADERS.
THEY WERE STIRRED BY BURNING FIRES OF
WONDER AND CURIOSITY, AND THEIR PURSUIT
OF KNOWLEDGE SOWED THE SEEDS TO MAKE
THEIR OWN SOCIETIES, AND OUR WORLD,
A BETTER PLACE.

# FOURTH AND FIFTH CENTURIES

# HYPATIA

## PHILOSOPHER QUEEN

Hypatia's heroism lies not in the brutality that she suffered at the end of her life, but in the subtle barriers she overcame each day while she lived.

—Edward J. Watts, *Hypatia: The Life and Legend of an Ancient Philosopher*

The woman we know as Hypatia, a highly esteemed mathematician and philosopher, is almost certainly a legend. When we dig through the dusty layers of history and myth into what we truly know about her, it turns out that it's not an awful lot. The stories that have been told are cloaked in so many embellishments that sixteen centuries after she lived, it's impossible to know what is true and what is hyperbole. Hypatia, like so many intellectual and brilliant women, exists in the modern era as an example of what can happen when women's writings, creative endeavors, and scholastic achievements are lost to time and the tyranny of low expectations. If students learn about this fascinating figure today, it's almost certainly in the context of her gruesome death at the hands of a bloodthirsty fifth-century Christian mob. But what about her life? What about her work?

The fact that we know more about how Hypatia died than how she lived is both sad and ironic because based on what historians have been able to piece together, she led a pretty remarkable life. She was born into the intellectual elite of Roman-occupied Alexandria in what is now Egypt, and although the exact year of her birth is unknown, many educated guesses place it around 355 CE.

There is no record of her mother or any siblings, but we do know her father: Theon, also a mathematician and philosopher. Hypatia's early education in this rarefied atmosphere at her father's knee was rigorous and deep. At this time mathematics interwove the study of philosophy and astronomy, and Hypatia took a strong interest in how these seemingly disparate subjects informed each other. Learning philosophy wasn't just an academic program, but

SHE WAS SO STRONGLY DEDICATED TO LIVING THE PURE LIFE DEMANDED BY HER PHILOSOPHICAL BELIEFS THAT WHEN ONE OF HER STUDENTS FELL IN LOVE WITH HER, SHE TRIED TO TEACH HIM TO RESIST HIS URGES THROUGH MUSIC.

rather a lifelong commitment to mastering contemplative understanding, which was thought to bring one closer to the divine. The particular Platonic philosophy that Hypatia taught and practiced "emphasized that unity with God could be achieved through contemplation rather than ritual."[12]

Eventually, Hypatia is believed to have exceeded Theon's own knowledge and took over teaching students throughout the city. She cut a stately figure and was always dressed in the academic robes traditionally reserved for men. She opened her educational sessions to the public to anyone who wished to learn—within limits. Alexandria was a city divided by strong class lines. As a member of the elite classes, Hypatia would only have taught those from her own social strata. So when historians say she taught the public, we must assume that the poor and lower classes were not allowed into these "public" lectures. As was common for philosophers during this time, Hypatia also had a small private circle of disciples that she taught over several years. Their education would have been much more thorough and in depth. This created what some call an "intellectual family," where students would sometimes refer to her as "mother."

A few other female philosophers and esteemed teachers are documented in this period, but Hypatia was revered for her "purity" and her lifelong virginity, which provided the social cover she needed to teach men privately. She was so strongly dedicated to living the pure life demanded by her philosophical beliefs that when one of her students fell in love with her, she tried to teach him to resist his urges through music. Not surprisingly, that failed to have an effect. She then reportedly showed her student her menstrual rags to demonstrate the impurity of the body and illustrate how fleeting physical love was compared to "divine, philosophical love." (Yeah, we think that's pretty bizarre as well.)

Anecdotes like this illuminate just a little bit of how gendered Hypatia's experiences as an instructor would have been. Sadly, none of Hypatia's own writings have survived to our current era. Our modern understanding of this great philosopher is carefully pieced together through letters from former students and others who lived during her time and directly after. Since everything we know about Hypatia comes from texts written by men, we can't know anything about the struggles she faced as a woman in a male-dominated field.

A FEW OTHER FEMALE PHILOSOPHERS AND ESTEEMED TEACHERS ARE DOCUMENTED IN THIS PERIOD, BUT HYPATIA WAS REVERED FOR HER "PURITY" AND HER LIFELONG VIRGINITY, WHICH PROVIDED THE SOCIAL COVER SHE NEEDED TO TEACH MEN PRIVATELY.

Yet, based on what we know about the life and culture of Alexandria during the fourth and fifth centuries, we can shade in some details about the environment in which she must have existed. Contrary to how we tend to view the roles of women in the distant past, Hypatia was actually very respected and influential in Alexandria's government and politics. She consorted with civic leaders and the city's elite. When foreign notables were visiting Alexandria, she was often their first visit.

But around the 380s, the political climate in Alexandria began to change as the emperors in Rome withdrew support of pagan practices in favor of Christianity.

While there had always been some hostility between Christians and non-Christians—the pagans, who believed in multiple gods, and folks of the Jewish faith—the violence between them grew exponentially in the fifth century due to two important figures. Cyril had just become head of the Christian church in Alexandria after his uncle died in 412. He was power hungry and wanted to cement the church's authority in the city. This conflicted with Orestes, Alexandria's prefect and chief representative of Roman authority. Although baptized Christian, Orestes didn't believe that religious laws should dictate governing policies. Hypatia and Orestes were colleagues, and it's believed that Hypatia advised Orestes, among many others, on political and philosophical matters. A number of church-ordered attacks, such as the expulsion of Jewish people from the city, the destruction of important pagan statues, and even an attack on Orestes himself, exacerbated the tension.

Cyril, realizing that Hypatia held tremendous political influence, began a smear campaign to sway public opinion against the beloved philosopher. And while the elite ruling class was fond of Hypatia, the commoners either didn't know or didn't care about her. In this deeply superstitious time, Cyril just needed to claim that she was a witch and was using magic to control Orestes. This was enough to mobilize the populace against Hypatia.

According to letters written by a former student of hers, in March 415 a mob, led by a man named Peter, surrounded Hypatia's carriage and dragged her out and into a church. Stories vary about the particulars of her death. The unadorned version is that she was murdered after being attacked with shards of pottery, but in some of the more lurid accounts of her death, horrific detail is piled on horrific detail, including rape, eye gouging, and dismemberment. While the specific gruesome details of Hypatia's death are debatable, there is no question that it was barbaric. Her body (or pieces of her body) were taken to a nearby town and burned.

Hypatia had no children and no surviving extended family to ensure that a complete picture of her life and work was passed down through history. Her legacy as a scholar and philosopher is sadly incomplete. But based on what we do know of this remarkable woman, we suspect she would be devastated to learn that our lasting memory of her is a politically motivated murder rather than the decades she committed to mastering a life of philosophic purity.

# FATIMA AL-FIHRI

## MOTHER OF THE CHILDREN

A vast and imposing center of higher learning, paneled in intricate mosaic tiles and dark wood, sits beneath rows of precise arches in Fès, Morocco. Al-Qarawīyīn is the oldest continuously operational university in the world. The list of influential scientists and religious leaders associated with it is truly staggering, and includes figures like the Jewish philosopher Maimonides and explorer Leo Africanus. And it all stands as the legacy of a ninth-century Muslim woman named Fatima al-Fihri.

Fatima al-Fihri was born in Kairouan, in present-day Tunisia, to a merchant named Mohammed Abdullah al-Fihri. As a young girl, she moved with her family to Fès, a growing and cosmopolitan city of traders, scholars, religious leaders, poets, and artists. In this cultural mecca her father prospered, and the devout Fatima was educated and later married. Sadly, her husband and father died in fairly close succession, and she and her sister, Mariam, inherited a vast fortune.

It was al-Fihri's vision to use her inheritance to serve her faith. Fès's growing population had outpaced the number and size of the local mosques. So in 859 she chose Fès, her adopted home, as the site of the mosque that would eventually become al-Qarawīyīn University. Al-Qarawīyīn University was (and still remains) world-renowned. Students were taught theology, grammar, rhetoric, logic, medicine, mathematics, and astronomy.

It is startling for people who do not

know much about Islam to realize the emphasis it places on study and knowledge. The pursuit of knowledge and devotion to academic study are core principles of the Islamic faith. The Koran tells us that the first word of Allah to the prophet Muhammad was *iqra*, "read." It was this divine mandate that drove Fatima and her sister, who founded another mosque in Fès, to use their wealth to serve Allah, strengthening Islam among its believers. Fatima was celebrated by her contemporaries for directly overseeing the construction and development of the facility she was building to serve them. The founding of al-Qarawīyīn's madrassa, or religious school, was a high point of what's often called the Islamic Golden Age, which took place roughly between the eighth and thirteenth centuries.

The importance of al-Qarawīyīn to the city of Fès was immense. By the tenth century, other mosques in Fès would only sound their own *adhān*, the Muslim call to prayer, after they heard the one from al-Qarawīyīn. The impact of this storied institution continues to be felt today. It is vital that we recognize the importance of Muslim women to the dissemination of their faith and respective cultures. Superficial and stereotypical depictions of Muslims in Western media have little use for Muslim women

IT IS INCONCEIVABLE TO MANY WESTERNERS THAT MUSLIM WOMEN, OR MUSLIMAHS, COULD BE VOLUNTARILY DEVOTED TO THEIR FAITH—NOT BLINDLY, BUT WITH OPEN EYES.

because they do not easily fit into the preconceived notions of orientalist savages or rabid suicide bombers. If Muslim women are depicted at all, it is often to pay the barest lip service to their "subjugation" and "oppression." It is inconceivable to many Westerners that Muslim women, or Muslimahs, could be voluntarily devoted to their faith—not blindly, but with open eyes.

In a touching note, this storied institution is coming full circle as a testament to the skills and brilliance of women. Al-Qarawīyīn was founded by a woman of color, and recently a female architect and engineer completed the restoration of its ancient library. It has always been the work of women to revive and restore the work of other female scholars, to pave a path for any who want to learn. Fatima al-Fihri became known as Oum al-Banin (Mother of the Children), and we can think of no more fitting title for the woman who helped give birth to a rich climate of learning.

# FOURTEENTH CENTURY

## NOVELLA D'ANDREA

# BEHIND THE VEIL

In many ways, the story of fourteenth-century legal scholar Novella d'Andrea—or at least what we can reconstruct of it—is actually the story of many women. There is fourteenth-century courtly poet Christine de Pisan, who took Novella's life as a subject in one of her works. Beside Pisan is Bettisia Gozzadini, an early Italian legal scholar who predated Novella by about a century, but with whom Novella is often confused. And woven into the tapestry is Novella's sister, Bettina d'Andrea, who taught law at the University of Padua. And so on and so on. Novella d'Andrea's story is the story of many other women who managed to make a mark in medieval European letters. She is part of a small but significant community of early female intellectuals whose brilliance has been lost to history. They exist in our memories—if they exist at all—behind a kind of hazy veil of uncertainty. We can sense the general outlines of their lives, but really, all we truly have is an impression.

The gauzy, insubstantial film through which we must view these great thinkers is a striking metaphor because it parallels one of the most famous anecdotes about Novella d'Andrea: She was so beautiful that she had to teach from behind a veil so as not to distract her students. It's a compelling image, regardless of whether or not it's strictly true. As it happens, the same story is told of several other female scholars in history.

# BY AGE NINETEEN, NOVELLA WAS ACCOMPLISHED ENOUGH AS A JURIST TO TAKE OVER HER FATHER'S CLASSES AT THE UNIVERSITY OF BOLOGNA.

What is important is not that we take the story at face value, but that we pay attention to what it might reveal. Perhaps the emphasis on these women's "overwhelming beauty" is really about making sure that these women—who had stepped out of the domestic space and into a male-dominated academic one—nevertheless retained their femininity in a socially acceptable way. Perhaps Novella d'Andrea did teach from behind a veil—not because her beauty would be distracting, but the mere fact of her gender might be.

Novella d'Andrea was born in 1312 into a household of scholarly reflection and critical debate. She was the daughter of Giovanni d'Andrea, a famous scholar of canon law, and his educated wife, Milanzia. It's reported that by age nineteen, the brilliant and well-spoken Novella was accomplished enough as a jurist in her own right to take over her father's classes at the University of Bologna in his absence.

Seem improbable? Not particularly.

Although their numbers were small, we do find women holding professorships in medieval Italy. For instance, during the late medieval period the celebrated medical school of Salerno boasted a contingent of female professors, including its entire department of "women's diseases," or what we would now call gynecology. Novella and her sister, Bettina d'Andrea, stepped into this tradition.

Despite the little we know about Novella, she remains a compelling figure across the ages. Historians continue to seek out the traces of her life, and writers pen narratives trying to fill in the gaps. Her story inspired Christine de Pisan, whose fervent celebration of women, *The Book of the City of Ladies*, is perhaps most responsible for our modern understanding of Novella's life.

What we don't know about Novella is, in some ways, as striking as what we do know. We know that she married, although sources differ about whether her husband was Giovanni Calderini or someone else. We know that she died young, but even the date of her passing is up for debate. She doesn't leave any notable writings that we can excavate for details about how her phenomenal mind worked. Novella, like so many brilliant women before her, remains lost to history, shrouded behind a veil that we cannot easily brush aside.

# WANG ZHENYI

## THE EVENING STAR

It's made to believe,

Women are the same as Men;

Are you not convinced,

Daughters can also be heroic?

— WANG ZHENYI

Under a canopy of stars, contemplating the inky vastness of the night's sky, we can truly feel a part of the majesty of the cosmos. The wonder of the stars, planets, and moon inspired eighteenth-century Qing Dynasty poet and astronomer Wang Zhenyi, and through her work, she has passed down a bit of that wonder to the generations following her.

Born into a family of scholars in 1768, Zhenyi grew up surrounded by books and the desire to learn everything that someone could teach her. Her grandfather was a former provincial governor and a noted book collector. He had seventy-five cases filled with books—something that would be remarkable today, let alone in the eighteenth century, before the advent of cheap printing. Zhenyi's grandfather sparked her curiosity and taught her astronomy. Her grandmother taught her poetry, and her father taught her medicine, geography, and mathematics. Zhenyi possessed an insatiable curiosity, also spending time learning

ZHENYI POSSESSED AN INSATIABLE CURIOSITY, ALSO SPENDING TIME LEARNING MARTIAL ARTS, HORSEBACK RIDING, AND ARCHERY FROM THE WIFE OF A MONGOLIAN GENERAL.

martial arts, horseback riding, and archery from the wife of a Mongolian general.

It's hard to think of something she couldn't do.

She had a truly remarkable analytical mind, conceiving and executing brilliant experiments (including setting up a model in her family's garden pavilion to confirm the operation of solar and lunar eclipses).

But it was also important to Zhenyi to share the knowledge that she acquired. A voracious reader of complex, weighty tomes, she worked to simplify them for beginners and laypeople. Although she is credited with publishing twelve scientific works during her short life, only one source of her output survives, compiled after her death: *Shusuan jiancun* (Simple principles of calculation).

Zhenyi married a man named Zhan Mei when she was twenty-five, and although the marriage was reportedly a happy one, the change in her position required oversight of her new home. Only four years after her marriage, Zhenyi died for unknown reasons. Before her untimely death, she asked that her papers be passed to her close friend Madam Kuai, who in turn passed them on to her nephew, a celebrated scholar in his own right. His estimation of Zhenyi as an unparalleled intellect comes down to us from his writings about her.

The bulk of Zhenyi's work that survives is her poetry. This is not surprising. In many ways, poetry and letters were considered a more acceptable pursuit for women. Even without deliberate malice or suppression, it makes sense that Zhenyi's more stereotypically "feminine" pursuits are passed down as her most enduring legacy.

Venus, the brightest planet in the sky, is the only one named after a female deity. In 1994, a crater on Venus was named after Wang Zhenyi. When you look into the night sky, seek out Venus and be dazzled by the celestial body and the woman who saw the stars and felt the wonder of the universe.

# ANNIE EASLEY

## HUMAN COMPUTER

Against all odds, the human computer walked into the room.

It was 1955. Racist Jim Crow rules enforcing segregation were still the law of the land. And yet the face of America was changing. The nascent civil rights movement to end inequality was gathering steam. The traditional hierarchies that had so long served white men, to the exclusion of everyone else, were slowly, inexorably starting to crumble.

During World War II, many women who had been relegated to the home found a world of employment suddenly available to them. The war effort demanded a ready, willing, and able labor force to take the place of the men who had gone off to fight.

Women flooded into factories and warehouses to operate machinery, drive trucks, and work on assembly lines, their hair pinned back and sleeves rolled up. And what do you know? It turns out they were great at it.

Of course, many women of color had been working outside the home in grueling, physical jobs long before the war. The realities of their lives required their financial contribution to keep the family stable and fed. But as larger numbers of white women started to join them in the workforce, the demographics of American labor changed forever. Once American women escaped the confines of the home, many never went back. Women weren't only working as factory hands. A few found professional work. Enter Annie Easley, a walking computational machine and a black woman who was a vital part of the American conquest of outer space.

Annie Jean Easley was born in Birmingham, Alabama, on April 23, 1933. She was an excellent math student, but like many women of the time, she never considered that there was a way to make a career out of it. But Easley wasn't just a good student—she was also a stubborn one. Opinionated and sure of herself, Easley was often kept after class for "talking back." That kind of self-assurance would serve her well throughout her life.

After high school, Easley moved to New Orleans to attend Xavier University of Louisiana. She majored in pharmacy, but never finished her degree. Instead, she got married and headed to Cleveland, Ohio. Easley had every intention of resuming her pharmacy studies in Cleveland, but wasn't able to find a school within a reasonable distance. It was a loss for pharmaceutical science, but an immeasurable gain for aeronautics.

While living in Cleveland, Easley read a profile in the local newspaper about twin sisters who were employed as "computers" at a nearby research lab of the National Advisory Committee for Aeronautics. The

## EASLEY'S WORK WAS INSTRUMENTAL IN LAUNCHING ROCKETS INTO SPACE AND HELPING SCIENTISTS UNDERSTAND THE GALAXIES BETTER.

next day, she drove to the lab to check it out, and within two weeks she had a job. Easley remained there for thirty-four years.

During this time computers were actually people who did complex mathematical computations, sometimes with the aid of giant, unwieldy calculating machines, but just as often solving equations lightning fast and accurately in their heads. It's interesting to note that when men did the job of human computers, it was a position that commanded a great deal of respect and allowed them career advancement. Once women started to perform the exact same work, its importance diminished, and suddenly, it was considered "inferior" clerical work. Eventually electronic computers would take over, and human computers received new titles such as math technician or mathematician.

In 1958, when space exploration became a national priority, the Cleveland research lab was folded into the National Aeronautics and Space Administration. Over the next three decades, Easley's work was instrumental in launching rockets into space and helping scientists understand the galaxies better. This was a huge point of pride for her. The sheer breadth and depth of the projects she participated in is awe-inspiring. Early on, Easley ran simulations for the building of NASA's nuclear test reactor at Plum Brook. She tested technology to collect and analyze data from the ozone layer. As machines replaced the human computers, Easley became a programmer and wrote code used in space launches. She even developed code to analyze alternative power technology—including the battery technology that was used in early hybrid vehicles.

She was an eager and valued member of the NASA family, but let's not forget that being a black woman working in a technical field in the 1950s and '60s was not an easy path (nor is it today, for that matter). Easley had to navigate bias and discrimination as a woman of color in a field dominated by white men—but she refused to let it discourage her, and she continued to talk back, in the way she had since she was a child. She noted many years later that her attitude to the bigots around her was "You may control my purse strings, but you don't control my life."[13]

By the 1970s, things were continuing to improve for women in the workforce, but it was still far from a haven of equality. In an extensive oral history interview in the NASA archives, Easley remembered the first time she wore pants to work—still a big deal for women in professional settings at that point! So big a deal that she even discussed it with her supervisor. Easley and her supervisor made a pact that they would both wear pants to the office the next day. Starting immediately, more and more women arrived at work wearing pants. It seems like such a small thing, but it points to a larger issue of self-determination and independence.

Annie Easley retired in 1989, but her life after NASA didn't slow down. She was an avid volunteer, participating in professional women's groups as well as becoming the president of the local ski council in Cleveland. She even started a new career in real estate!

Annie Jean Easley passed away on June 25, 2011. Her life stands as an enduring testament to how opening doors for women elevates an entire society. Easley and the women she worked with—those marvelous human computers—made it possible for women everywhere to dream bigger and reach further. Annie Easley never really thought of herself as a role model. But we think she was.

# RUTHLESS VILLAINS

What do a Cantonese pirate, a fifteenth-century queen, and the

first female prime minister of the United Kingdom have in common?

A lot more than you would think. Read on.

It might seem odd to include a list of murderers, thieves, and spectacularly ruthless heads of state in a book celebrating women's long-forgotten achievements and accomplishments. But we don't think so. The feminist work of uncovering, restoring, and documenting the lives of women who have been erased from our histories should not be limited to those who fit our definitions of good and noble (definitions, by the way, that change significantly throughout time and across cultures).

The fight for true equality is not about female supremacy, nor is it about claiming that women are inherently more virtuous, ethical, or compassionate people. As the portraits in this book demonstrate, it's ridiculous to insist that women are inherently inferior, less intelligent, or less capable than men. Women have the same capacity for good and evil as all humans. Want

# PUTTING WOMEN ON A PEDESTAL IS REALLY JUST ANOTHER WAY TO KEEP THEM IN A BOX.

a simple definition for what feminism truly is? We think it doesn't get much better than this one from writer Marie Shear: "Feminism is the radical notion that women are people."

The dynamic, daring, and determined women within this book illustrate how smart, capable, and creative women can be. They brilliantly exemplify the ways that women around the world and throughout history have persevered, under enormous opposition, to make their mark and make a difference.

Sadly, some of the most unyielding opposition women face comes from outdated notions that claim to uplift us. This

often takes the form of stereotypical ideas about femininity: Women are nurturers. Women are inherently compassionate. Women are somehow more pure or virtuous.

On the face of it, these seem like positive traits. But when we take the time to really think them through, we realize that putting women on a pedestal is really just another way to keep them in a box. By only allowing women to express vague and restrictive qualities like "purity" or "morality," we deny them the full range of human feeling and behavior. And when the histories are written, we neglect any woman who refuses to stay in that restrictive box (even though so few of us actually fit).

Western society systematically excludes women from participating in the same full range of activities as men, so we don't really know what to make of ruthless, criminal women's personalities and actions. As a result, our imaginations are limited, and we deny ourselves a truly rich and complex understanding of who we are.

This section is dedicated to the women who are just as conniving, murderous, gruesome, horrifying, and uncomfortably fascinating as the men whose names we already know. For while we would like less evil in the world, we cannot be selective about what, and who, we choose to remember.

Are we advocating for an uncritical hero worship of the women in this section on female villainy? Far from it. What we would like to suggest, however, is that we can and must take out our pens and rewrite all kinds of women back into our stories. It is only by understanding that women are people—sometimes messy, flawed, awful people—that we can work to overcome the limitations that tell us to stay quiet, invisible, and out of the way while men go about the business of making history.

So how did we choose who to include in this section on villains, rogues, con-artists, and criminals?

FIRST: All the women here rose to the heights of power in traditionally male-dominated spheres. And all of them—from the seventeenth-century English highway robber Moll Cutpurse to the twentieth-century Iron Lady, Margaret Thatcher—used intimidation, violence, or ruthless control to maintain that power.

NEXT: These women had longevity. They grabbed power by the horns and wouldn't let go until forced to. Chinese pirate queen Ching Shih went from marauding on the high seas to cracking the whip over a gambling den. Griselda Blanco reigned over a cocaine empire so vast and deep that it stretched over two continents and even endured her numerous years in jail.

FINALLY: These women were fearless. Despite the overwhelming pressure for women to live quiet lives out of the spotlight, all the women in this section achieved fame—and in some cases, infamy—by being bold and unflinching in their pursuit of wealth, power, or greatness.

These are the stories of villains, rogues, and rascals who might frighten us, but who will carve their names—and crimes—into our memories.

## "FEMINISM IS THE RADICAL NOTION THAT WOMEN ARE PEOPLE."

# FIFTEENTH CENTURY

# ISABEL I

## QUEEN & COUNTRY

There are few monarchs whose legacy of good and evil weigh so heavily on history as that of Isabel I. The fifteenth-century Spanish queen ushered in an unparalleled era of wealth, power, and territorial expansion for her fractured nation. But counterbalancing the long column of her positive achievements is one glaring evil: the Inquisition—an unfathomable cruelty that she engineered against the Jewish and Muslim citizens of her land.

Born in 1451 to the second wife of Juan II of Castile, the young princess quickly demonstrated the abiding religious devotion and stern purpose that would guide her reign

as Isabella the Catholic. Despite living in comparative neglect once her father died and her half brother Enrique IV ascended to the throne, she dedicated herself to learning and prayer. In fact, her faith was the one constant in her young life. After her father's passing in 1454, her mother (also named Isabel) was forced to depend upon the kindness of fickle nobles for shelter and financial support, as the monies promised them by the terms of Juan II's will were perpetually blocked by King Enrique.

Rather than blossoming into a fairy-tale princess among the sumptuous luxury and fawning servants of the court, Isabel found herself seeking the stability of Mother

Church. She grew to adulthood fully molded—some would say *warped*—by clerical mentors who infused her with a brimstone-soaked understanding of divine judgment that was firmly wedded to a zealous nationalism. Christianity and citizenship—the two became synonymous.

Large numbers of Jewish and Muslim people had been part of the fabric of Spanish life for several hundred years before Isabel was born, but back in the seventh century, a concerted effort to dispel and eradicate the Jewish citizenry had begun to flower. Considering these people inauthentic or illegitimate citizens by reason of their heritage, Christian kings ordered conversion or exile for all Jewish citizens. Throughout the century, the Councils of Toledo, whose religious decrees were the law of the land, continued the persecution, eventually ordering enslavement for anyone still practicing Judaism. The arrival of Muslim conquerors in 711 restored Jewish life in the country, but as Christian monarchs reclaimed more and more territory over the centuries, anti-Semitism reemerged. By the time Isabel took the throne in 1474, anti-Semitic hatred and anti-Muslim fervor had been elevated to a virtue by those who wished to "preserve" Spain.

Inspired by Joan of Arc, who had been burned at the stake only two decades before

INSPIRED BY JOAN OF ARC, THE DEVOUT YOUNG PRINCESS MADE IT HER MISSION TO UNITE HER COUNTRY UNDER A CATHOLIC BANNER.

Isabel's birth, the devout young princess made it her mission to unite her country under a Catholic banner.

Although Isabel's fires were internal, their destructive energy was no less consuming. At age eighteen, Isabel married Fernando of Aragon, joining the two kingdoms. Her marriage was against the wishes of her brother the king, who had wanted to marry her off to further his own strategic ends. But King Enrique's power had long been on the wane, and Isabel was able to defy his wishes with the help of the church. Five years later, her brother died, and she became queen.

She and Fernando, los Reyes Católicos (the Catholic Sovereigns), initiated the infamous Spanish Inquisition. While it was not the only Inquisition in Europe, it was remarkably brutal, even by medieval standards. With Isabel's blessing, priests like Tomás de Torquemada spread terror throughout the land attempting to ensure orthodoxy and obedience to the church. Isabel's Inquisition consigned the broken bodies and souls of heretics (Muslims, Jews, "suspicious" converts, or anyone else who was perceived to flout the rigid lines of church dogma) to torment and agony. One group that was particularly singled out were women such as the conversas, the Jewish female converts who were accused of Judaizing or secretly abiding by the "false" doctrine of Judaism and maintaining Jewish cultural traditions. In an especially cruel irony, we may never know how many people died or were tortured by these powerful priests. Although the inquisitorial officers kept detailed records of their proceedings, many of those records, like the lives they represented, are lost.

So how do we understand a woman—a ruler—like Isabel? Independence and autonomy are never easy to achieve, and ambitious women are rarely honored without reservation. Isabel stands out as a powerful woman and a ruler who inspired incredible admiration. Her support for Christopher Columbus and other explorers led to an explosion in Spanish wealth and global influence. And yet in 1492, the same year that "Christopher Columbus sailed the ocean blue," Isabel and Fernando signed their names to the infamous Alhambra Decree, which called for the expulsion or conversion of all Spanish Jews.

The consolidation of Isabel's kingdom and the expansion of her empire—like all empires—was built upon subjugation and oppression. It came on the heels of the vicious treatment of tens of thousands of her subjects. In the name of God and country, "Isabella the Catholic" (a title bestowed on her by the pope himself, and the way she thereafter signed her papers) evangelized an uncompromising version of Christian citizenship until the day she died in 1504. She was a steadfast true believer. In the end, we can best understand the legacy of Isabel by wrestling with her own understanding of divine inspiration, which she explained to the pope during the war against the Muslims in Granada:

It is certain and well known that we have not been moved nor are we moved to this war for the accumulation of more kingdoms, nor greed to acquire more rents than what we already have, nor a desire to accumulate treasures. All this we could do, if we indeed wanted to, with much less danger, work and expenses than this war is creating for us. But the desire that we have for the service of God and zeal for the Holy Catholic Faith makes us do this.[14]

# MOLL CUTPURSE

## THE ROARING GIRL

I've never robbed any poor man yet
Nor any tradesman caused I to fret
But I robbed Lords and their Ladies fine
And I carried their gold home to my heart's delight

—"THE NEWRY HIGHWAYMAN"
(traditional Irish folk song)

W e've never known what to do with bad girls. To be honest, no one knows what to do with girls in general, but bad girls—now, that's even more of a difficulty. Bad girls don't fit into boxes, and they won't answer when called. They refuse to do what they're told or to play with the right toys.

Mary Frith, aka Moll Cutpurse, was that kind of girl. She was fiercely, unapologetically her own person—and she was completely unwilling to be bound by social expectations for "good girls." She cut a dashing and scandalous figure through seventeenth-century England, riding around in men's clothes, fencing stolen goods, and generally living the life of a boisterous, smoking, straight-talking rogue. She inspired comic plays and bawdy songs, and her name was shouted as a warning to other women to behave.

Oh, she was a wild one. Running rampant and wanton as a child on the streets of London, young Mary drove her family to distraction early. Left to the horrified stares of a disapproving public, we would know only this about her:

> She was above all breeding and instruction. She was a very tomrig or hoyden, and delighted only in boys' play and pastime, not minding or companying with the girls. Many a bang and blow this hoyting procured her, but she was not so to be tamed, or taken off from her rude inclinations. She could not endure that sedentary life of sewing or stitching; a sampler was as grievous to her as a winding sheet; and on her needle, bodkin and thimble she could not think quietly, wishing them changed into sword and dagger for a bout at cudgels.[15]

On the other hand, does that really sound so bad? Despite the uncertainty of some particulars of Moll's biography, there is one thing of which we can be sure: From the beginning of her life, she refused to comport herself according to the strictly regimented expectations of womanhood at the time and chose instead to play, work, and live the way she wanted.

And what exactly was that life like? Well, Mary was an only child who was doted on by her mother, so despite driving her family to distraction, she did not suffer from a complete absence of love and affection as a child. Still, it's clear that her desire to exercise the same freedom as young men provoked worry and consternation. As she grew older and her behavior could no longer be excused by the wildness of youth, her uncle tried to ship her off to America for a presumably rehabilitative stay in the colonies. On board the westward-bound frigate, when Mary realized where she was headed, it's said that she jumped overboard and swam for shore!

Mary Frith never lacked for a certain kind of reckless courage throughout her life. She began her criminal career fairly young (by sixteen, she'd already been arrested for stealing money), and she dabbled in a whole host of illicit activity, including time as a highwayman (or rather highwaywoman). Her nickname, Moll Cutpurse, in fact, came from her supposed method of thievery:

HER NICKNAME, MOLL CUTPURSE, IN FACT, CAME FROM HER SUPPOSED METHOD OF THIEVERY: WORKING WITH A PARTNER WHO DISTRACTED THE VICTIMS, MOLL WOULD SNIP THE STRINGS OF THEIR PURSES OFF THEM, "CUTTING THEIR PURSE."

Working with a partner who distracted the victims, Moll would snip the strings of their purses off them, "cutting their purse." But no matter how many times Moll was caught and punished for her criminal activities—she went to prison more than once and had her hands branded, a common punishment for thieves—Moll never reformed. When one form of crime proved too dangerous, she simply switched to another. After being nicked for a daring highway robbery of General Thomas Fairfax, and in danger of being hanged at the gallows, Moll paid 2,000 pounds to get out of jail and simply switched from active thievery to receiving other folks' stolen goods. One can only imagine the amount of stress and worry she caused the forces of authority around her: Not only was she too clever and too tireless to stay on the right side of the law, she flaunted her independence by gamboling around town, smoking and drinking with men in public—while wearing men's clothes, to boot.

It was, in fact, her refusal to wear "proper" women's clothes that rankled many people the most.

During one of her many brushes with the outraged London authorities, Moll was sentenced to stand in the open-air pulpit outside Saint Paul's Cathedral during an entire Sunday sermon wearing nothing but a white sheet. This was meant to humiliate and silence her, but once again, Moll proved irrepressible:

> An Accusation [was] exhibited against me for wearing indecent and manly apparel. . . . I was sentenced there to stand and do Penance in a White Sheet at Pauls Cross during morning Sermon on a Sunday.
>
> They might as soon have shamed a Black Dog as Me, with any kind of such punishment; for saving the reverence due to those who enjoyed it, for a halfe-penny I would have Travelled to all the Market Towns in England with it.[16]

By the end of her life, Moll's sizable criminal empire had faded somewhat, and seven decades of hard drinking, smoking, and large living had taken their toll on her physically. We should also not discount the relentless pressure of social expectations that weighed upon older women of this period. Moll never married and never had children. There was no social safety net to take care of her, or family to whom she could turn for care—if, indeed, she would have wanted to. We simply can't know what Moll thought near the end of her life, as age and riotous living slowly consumed her body. What we do know is that she spent time in Bethlehem Hospital, afflicted with mental doubts and instability. She was eventually released, "cured" of her "insanity." In 1659, she died as she lived, as a figure of renown. No less a person than the esteemed English poet John Milton wrote her epitaph:

> FOR NO COMMUNION SHE HAD,
> NOR SORTED WITH
> THE GOOD OR BAD;
> THAT WHEN THE WORLD
> SHALL BE CALCIN'D,
> AND THE MIX'D MASS
> OF HUMAN KIND
> SHALL SEP'RATE BY
> THAT MELTING FIRE,
> SHE'LL STAND ALONE,
> AND NONE COME NIGH HER.[17]

# NINETEENTH CENTURY

# LADY DESTINY

When most people think of pirates, they imagine hulking, fearsome men with names like Blackbeard or Long John Silver. Although the vast majority of pirates throughout history have been male, one of the most famous and feared pirates who ever lived was Ching Shih, a young Cantonese woman who became the ruler of one of the largest pirate fleets in history and the mastermind behind a floating criminal empire so powerful that even the Chinese military couldn't stop it.

We don't know much about her early life, except that at one point she worked at a brothel in Canton. In 1801, Ching Shih married a pirate commander named Ching Yih and soon ruled by his side as he expanded his empire, unifying countless small scattered crews of pirates into an organized and increasingly powerful coalition. When her husband died suddenly in 1807, Ching Shih knew exactly what to do: She stepped in to claim the leadership for herself—taking control of somewhere between forty thousand and sixty thousand pirates.

Their acceptance of a woman as their commander remains a remarkable testament to both her political skill and the respect she must have earned from the crew. She soon appointed her adopted son, Chang Pao, as the commander of her most powerful fleet and eventually married him. It

was a little creepy, but the two became a formidable team whose raids were feared throughout the South China Sea.

We don't know exactly what Ching looked like, although some historians have assumed she caught the eye of her pirate husband through good looks rather than her considerable intelligence. While there are flamboyant but dubious accounts invented by Western writers of a gorgeous "goddess" wielding swords and wearing glittering battle gear covered in golden dragons, more reliable texts describe Ching Shih as "a good military strategist," a "strict disciplinarian," and "an excellent businesswoman." This much was true.

Although she rejected many traditional ideas about what women could and couldn't do, other rules were extremely important—namely those enforced on her ships. With

the help of a code of conduct drawn up by Chang Pao, she established clear rules for the behavior, finances, and power structure of the fleet, as well as the draconian punishments that awaited anyone who dared to disobey or cheat her. Her rule was unquestionably harsh, not only for the victims of her raids, but for anyone in her fleet who dared to step out of line.

Among the rules that Ching Shih imposed was that all plunder had to be registered, with 80 percent of the loot paid into a general fund. Somewhat ironically, stealing from the fund was one of the worst crimes a pirate could commit, and the punishment was death. As one observer noted, Ching Shih's strict and often lethal reaction to misbehavior kept the crew very honest, and the pirates under her command "took great care to behave themselves well."

Through careful and ruthless management, Ching Shih made the bloody and chaotic work of piracy into a highly organized business, and business was good, making her a very wealthy woman.

And of course, like so many male leaders, conquerors, and generals throughout history, her prosperity and success came at the cost of innocent lives. Her remarkable story is a reminder that regardless of the

# CHING SHIH MADE THE BLOODY AND CHAOTIC WORK OF PIRACY INTO A HIGHLY ORGANIZED BUSINESS, AND BUSINESS WAS GOOD.

# LIKE SO MANY MALE LEADERS, HER PROSPERITY AND SUCCESS CAME AT THE COST OF INNOCENT LIVES.

limitations placed on them, women can be anything that men can be: brilliant and brutal, courageous and cruel, powerful and dreadful.

The Chinese government devoted considerable effort to crushing the pirates, but thanks in large part to Ching Shih's strategic skill, her fleets became so powerful that the government eventually stopped trying to destroy them and started negotiating with them instead.

Ching Shih knew that piracy was not a career built for longevity, especially when the most common retirement plan was death. So, in 1810 she stepped off a boat and, surrounded by the wives and children of her pirates, walked completely unarmed to the office of the local governor-general to discuss amnesty.

With a fearsome floating army at her back, Ching Shih negotiated a very good deal: Not only were she and any other pirates who surrendered completely pardoned by the government for their many, many crimes, but they kept all their ill-gotten plunder and even received jobs from the government if they wanted. Her husband gained a position in the military as a lieutenant, where he commanded a private fleet—made up of former pirates, of course.

Thanks to her exceptional cunning and bravery, Ching Shih ended her life of piracy not as a criminal behind bars or the casualty of a raid gone wrong, but rather by gathering her riches and retiring in comfort as a law-abiding citizen. Well, mostly law-abiding. She spent her later years running a gambling establishment back in Canton, where she reportedly led a "peaceful life," or at least as peaceful as she could manage while presiding over a notorious gambling den.

When she finally died in 1844 at sixty-nine years old, she had transformed herself from a relatively powerless young woman into the most powerful female pirate in history, plus something almost as rare: a pirate who died from old age.

# GRISELDA BLANCO

## CALL ME GODMOTHER

The crack and pop. Shots. Bangs. The snap and the blow.

America in the 1970s and '80s discoed to a bloody soundtrack: a booming, staccato beat of gun violence and drive-by shootings, urban decline and quick hits. Dead bodies and no witnesses.

It was the era of big hair, big money, and most of all, it was the era of cocaine.

And rising from those mountains of white powder was a queen: Griselda Blanco. La Madrina. By the time she was brutally gunned down in 2012, La Madrina had amassed a fortune of over a billion dollars by trafficking cocaine to the United States for the Medellín drug cartel. She was rumored to have been responsible for over two hundred murders, personally pulling the trigger countless times. The first time was the merciless murder of a well-to-do young boy who had been kidnapped for ransom.

She was eleven years old.

Born in 1943 to a mother whose descent into alcoholism precipitated brutal beatings, Griselda Blanco escaped from her home in Medellín at the age of fourteen and fell deeper into the welcoming arms of the underworld. By the time she left home, she had been exploited as a child prostitute for three years. The world she inhabited was painted in shades of misery everywhere she looked, with two cardinal rules: Take what you can. Survive at all costs. They were brutal lessons, but ones that eventually guided Blanco to the

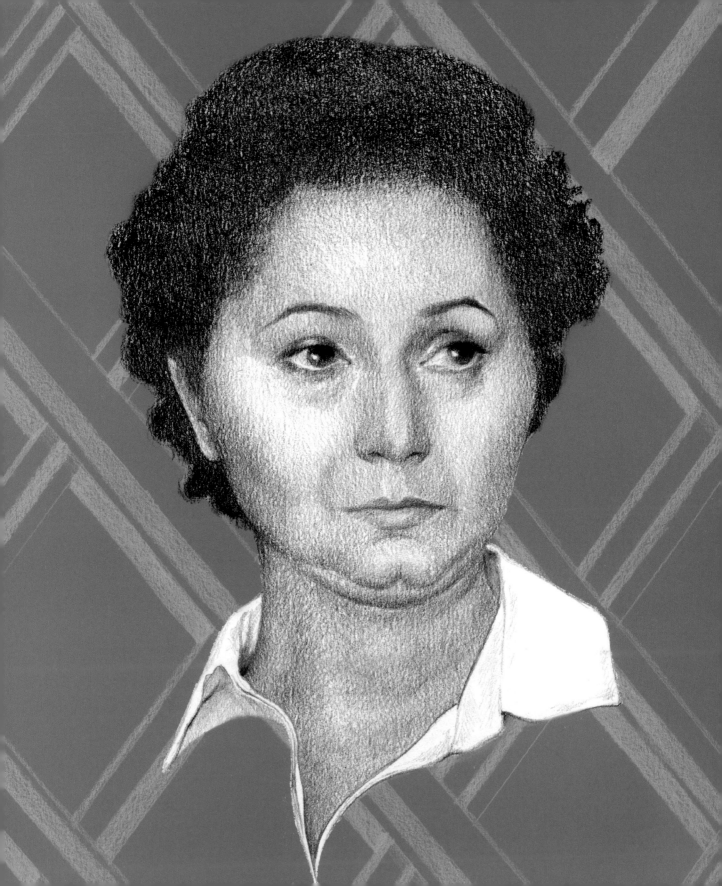

# BLANCO MADE A BREAK FOR COLOMBIA, BUT THE LURE OF A COCAINE COWBOY'S FAT MONEY AND LAVISH LIFESTYLE WAS TOO MUCH TO RESIST.

top of a criminal empire that stretched from Colombia to New York, from Peru to Miami.

Blanco's first marriage was to a young forger and hustler named Carlos Trujillo. Griselda and Carlos had three children together, but eventually divorced. Carlos made two crucial errors during his marriage: First, he introduced his wife to Alberto Bravo, the man who would become Blanco's next husband, and second, he failed to show his wife the respect she demanded. Several stories circulate about what happened to Carlos, but many people believe that for the latter mistake, Carlos had a hit taken out on him by Blanco herself. And thus was born the legend of the Black Widow.

As it happens, Blanco's second husband, Alberto, would ultimately suffer a premature end as well. Whether or not Blanco pulled the trigger herself, as one government witness claims, Alberto Bravo's brutal death only bolstered Blanco's fearsome reputation as a cold-blooded woman to be reckoned with.

But before things came to such a brutal pass and while things were still good between them, Bravo and Blanco moved from Colombia to New York. They quickly established themselves as naturals in the drug trade, and business boomed. Business was so good, in fact, that Blanco was indicted on federal drug-trafficking charges in 1975. She made a break for Colombia, but the lure of a cocaine cowboy's fat money and lavish lifestyle was too much to resist. By 1979, Blanco was back in the United States and running things—but this time, she was going all out in the sun-soaked southern climes of Miami, Florida.

Before the Miami elites developed a craving for the expensive powder that Griselda and those like her were importing by the literal ton, Miami was known as a fairly sleepy, rather gauche haven for retirees. Marijuana was big, but it was cheap and rarely caused more than a ripple in the community and among law enforcement. But once the doctors, lawyers, and athletes of the area got a taste of the effects of cocaine, things began to shift rapidly. The money started coming in faster than people could spend it. Many of Miami's skyscrapers were reportedly built with laundered funds from the overwhelming influx of drug money.

And in the center of it all was Griselda Blanco. It was in Miami that the depths of her ruthlessness and the creativity of her cruelty really began to shine. Maybe it was because Griselda was starting to abuse the same drugs with which she was blanketing the city. What's undeniable is that Griselda became known for her brutality, coldness, and savagery in shoring up power. She was known for killing people to whom she owed money, as well as people who owed money to her. She would take out hits on people for something as seemingly insignificant as insulting a member of her family, and often those hits would come in the form of motorcycle drive-bys, a murder method that Griselda pioneered. A submachine gun shooting in broad daylight that killed two people and injured two bystanders at the Dadeland Mall was her handiwork. Law enforcement was stunned at the planning she had engineered to take out her rivals: a reinforced-steel "war wagon," equipped with gun ports, automatic weapons, thousands of rounds of ammunition, and bulletproof vests.

For a few years in Miami, Griselda seemed untouchable. Life was filled with extravagant parties that seemed as if they would never end. But the long arm of the law almost caught up to her there, too. Once again, she had to move.

Blanco ended up in Irvine, California, where her pedestal began to slowly crumble. In 1985, she was apprehended by DEA agent Bob Palombo and spent the next thirteen years in prison on federal drug charges before pleading guilty in Florida to three murders. But even in prison, Blanco cut a glamorous figure. There were no drab prison khakis for her—she wore silk pantsuits and heels and had drugs and specialty foods smuggled in. She might not have had her freedom, but she was still in charge. She continued to oversee her vast drug empire via surrogates and maintained her iron grip on the business.

Blanco even attempted to engineer the kidnapping of John F. Kennedy Jr. to extort the United States government into releasing her from prison and allowing her to return to Colombia. The plan failed, however, and she was not released from prison until 2004. Blanco was immediately deported back to Colombia, and it was there, in 2012, that she died in a motorcycle drive-by shooting—the same way so many of her enemies had gone before.

America has a fascination with mob stories and tales of outlaws, bandits, rogues, and villains. The cocaine cowboys satisfied our national need for a mind-altering fix, but also our desire for stories of larger-than-life figures who seem to have the world on a string. Griselda Blanco was every bit as ruthless and cruel as the fictional dons in movies like Scarface and *The Godfather*—and she relished these comparisons. She even named her youngest son Michael Corleone, after the heir apparent in *The Godfather*. When her son Osvaldo was killed by gang members in Medellín, La

## "TO THE COWARDS WHO KILLED MY SON, THE GROUND WILL SHAKE BENEATH YOUR FEET. THIS DEED WILL NOT GO UNPUNISHED."

Madrina sent a message from jail to be read by the priest at the funeral: "To the cowards who killed my son, the ground will shake beneath your feet. This deed will not go unpunished."[18]

Griselda Blanco lived by the sword, and that's how she died. She was sixty-nine years old and had spent over half a century building a criminal empire through terror and sheer force of will. Like the black widow, she drew others into her web and made them feed her vast hunger. Like Ching Shih before her, she expanded the illegal enterprises that brought her tremendous wealth and ran a tight, disciplined ship. Although neither of these women will go down in history as good people, they were undeniably fearsome leaders.

# MARGARET THATCHER

## THE ENEMY WITHIN

Powerful people attract us with their strength and decisiveness, and all too often, we begin to honor power for its own sake. We fail to truly reckon with the horrific effects that immense power can wreak on actual human lives. But know this: True power is almost always accompanied by the suffering of a society's vulnerable and voiceless members. Such is the case with the prolonged global influence wielded by UK prime minister Margaret Thatcher in the latter part of the twentieth century. When the history books honor her as the first female prime minister in all of Europe, when they tout her tenure as the United Kingdom's longest continuously serving prime minister in recent memory, when they

rewrite the truth to depict her as the savior of a weak national economy and a loyal champion of "British values," know this: People suffered. People died. Lives were ruined, and communities were torn apart.

Margaret Thatcher is directly responsible for trumped-up arrests of leftist activists and for the despair of thousands who could not feed their families or walk the streets safely because they were gay or immigrants. When we remember her, never forget that Margaret Hilda Thatcher, the one they called the Iron Lady, strode the marble halls of government in her tailored clothes and dowager hats, deaf to the echoing cries of any but the privileged few.

And yet despite all this, Margaret Thatcher

IT'S DIFFICULT TO OVERSTATE HOW POWERFUL
SHE WAS. THATCHERISM COMPLETELY
TRANSFORMED MODERN BRITISH POLITICS,
WITH THE RESULT THAT THE TWO PRIMARY
PARTIES AT PLAY, CONSERVATIVE AND LABOUR,
HAVE SOCIAL AND FINANCIAL POLICIES THAT
SEEM EFFECTIVELY IDENTICAL TO EACH OTHER.

continues to inspire fanatical hero worship among many British Conservatives even now, more than thirty years since she left office. The "me first" ethos she advocated—from the inhumane and violent suppression of long-standing labor unions to harmful industry deregulation—far outlasted her eleven years as prime minister and has come to be known as Thatcherism. It's difficult to overstate how powerful she was. Thatcherism completely transformed modern British politics, with the result that the two primary parties at play, Conservative and Labour, have social and financial policies that seem effectively identical to each other.

It's hard not to applaud when a woman demonstrates the kind of implacable will required to snatch power from male gate-keepers. To exert the kind of influence that changes world history demands an almost terrifying single-mindedness. But power is not in itself a virtue. The Iron Lady ascended the heights of power on the backs of the poor, the vulnerable, and the weak.

For a woman who eventually became one of the world's most powerful and most feared leaders, Margaret Hilda Roberts herself was born into comparatively modest circumstances: She was the daughter of a grocer, not an aristocrat. Her early school career was marked by persistence, tenacity, and relentless dedication to improvement, rather than brilliance or artistic talent. Her youth was solidly middle class, and the insistence on "pulling yourself up by your bootstraps" instilled in her a fervent belief in the virtue of pursuing wealth. She carried her middle-class aspirational upbringing throughout her political career, and it's undeniable that she is largely responsible for wresting the British Conservative Party from feeble and aristocratic "old boys" and recasting it as a party of vigorous, entrepreneurial anglers.

As a young woman, Thatcher graduated from Oxford with a degree in chemistry, and she was fiercely proud of her scientific training all her life. It was while she was at Oxford that she started to really lean into social conservatism and economic libertarianism, and she became president of the Oxford University Conservative Association in 1946. She had always been drawn to the law, and she qualified as a barrister in 1953—the same year she gave birth to her twin children, Mark and Carol. Being a young mother in any era is challenging, but Thatcher's drive led her to Parliament only six years later, in 1959. She flew the Conservative banner proudly, and her rise in party circles was steady and assured. Education secretary under Prime Minister Edward Heath in 1970. Leader of the Conservative Party by 1975. Prime minister

# THE IRON LADY ASCENDED THE HEIGHTS OF POWER ON THE BACKS OF THE POOR, THE VULNERABLE, AND THE WEAK.

in 1979. The Iron Lady emerged from her chrysalis and spread her wings on the world stage.

Her time in 10 Downing Street, the official residence of the UK prime minister (akin to the US White House), was controversial from the minute she crossed the threshold, but Thatcher held an almost preternatural self-possession and disregard for the opinion of others. She seemed . . . well, there's almost no word for it other than *unflappable*. When Northern Irish prisoners initiated a hunger strike in 1981, demanding they be treated as political prisoners rather than criminals, Thatcher allowed ten to die, showing little regard for them or their cause. During the Falklands War, her hawkish behavior could be seen as an illustration of her strategic prowess, but in the end her government was brutally indifferent to the actual human cost of the conflict and the men who returned from the war traumatized. The list goes on: She initiated the infamous poll tax that led to such massive unrest that hundreds of thousands converged on central London in 1990 to protest it. She seamlessly wove anti-immigrant rhetoric into her speeches, and her insistence on a very narrow definition of British "identity" was crucial in the Conservative effort to poach members from racist political organizations such as the National Front.

Nor can we forget Thatcher's tacit support of the racist, whites-only apartheid government in South Africa. While the rest of the world argued for and enforced eco-nomic sanctions designed to pressure South Africa's ruling National Party into long-overdue reform, Thatcher steadfastly refused to join their coalition. She characterized Nelson Mandela's African National Congress as a "typical terrorist organization," for its defiant activism to end apartheid rule and give voting rights to black and mixed-race citizens.

Complicating our understanding of Margaret Thatcher is that there are some issues where she was at least nominally on the right side of history. During her time as prime minister in the late 1980s, for instance, her speeches on climate change helped bring the issue into the mainstream. Early in her career, she took bold stances on certain social issues, such as the decriminalization of male homosexuality and abortion. Here, too, though, her record is stained. By the time she was at the height of her powers as prime minister, she ruled over a Conservative Party that employed horrifically homophobic rhetoric as a way to paint the Labour Party as inherently perverse and intent on corrupting the nation's youth. She oversaw the passing of Section 28, which outlawed the "promotion" of homosexuality in schools. The law never yielded a prosecution, but it effectively silenced educators,

## HER YOUTH WAS SOLIDLY MIDDLE CLASS, AND THE INSISTENCE ON "PULLING YOURSELF UP BY YOUR BOOTSTRAPS" INSTILLED IN HER A FERVENT BELIEF IN THE VIRTUE OF PURSUING WEALTH.

preventing them from speaking freely and openly with students about vital LGBT issues or providing the kind of sex education that would have saved lives during the AIDS crisis.

It is for all these things and more that Margaret Thatcher is such a problematic figure in world history, but especially women's history. Thatcher herself was not particularly interested in women's issues, and she would not have considered herself a feminist—no matter how insistently people try to grant her that label now. She led some in the United Kingdom to greater prosperity, but many others, including women in vulnerable circumstances, faced miserable deprivation and hardship. When Thatcher moved to ruthlessly suppress striking coal miners in 1984, she famously criticized them as if they were parasites, or foreign bodies. She scorned them as "the enemy within." In a way, that's what she represents to feminism. It is imperative that we look past her groundbreaking ascension to power and remember that her conservative policies and disregard for civil and labor rights were not unique and were very much in line with the actions of authoritarian, and male, world leaders.

For many, Margaret Thatcher is an

**THATCHER HELD AN ALMOST PRETERNATURAL SELF-POSSESSION AND DISREGARD FOR THE OPINION OF OTHERS. SHE SEEMED . . . WELL, THERE'S ALMOST NO WORD FOR IT OTHER THAN UNFLAPPABLE.**

irresistible figure: decisive, resolute, and supremely self-assured. Her power, like all power, has an allure. A seductive magnetism that draws us in and dazzles us, even when the use of that power against vulnerable people and communities is devastating and destructive. The legacy of powerful women like Margaret Thatcher illustrates how damaging it can be when we praise a woman for simply attaining, wielding, and maintaining power in a male-dominated space. Too many times, when we acknowledge her singularity, we gloss over the monstrous acts she may have committed to get there.

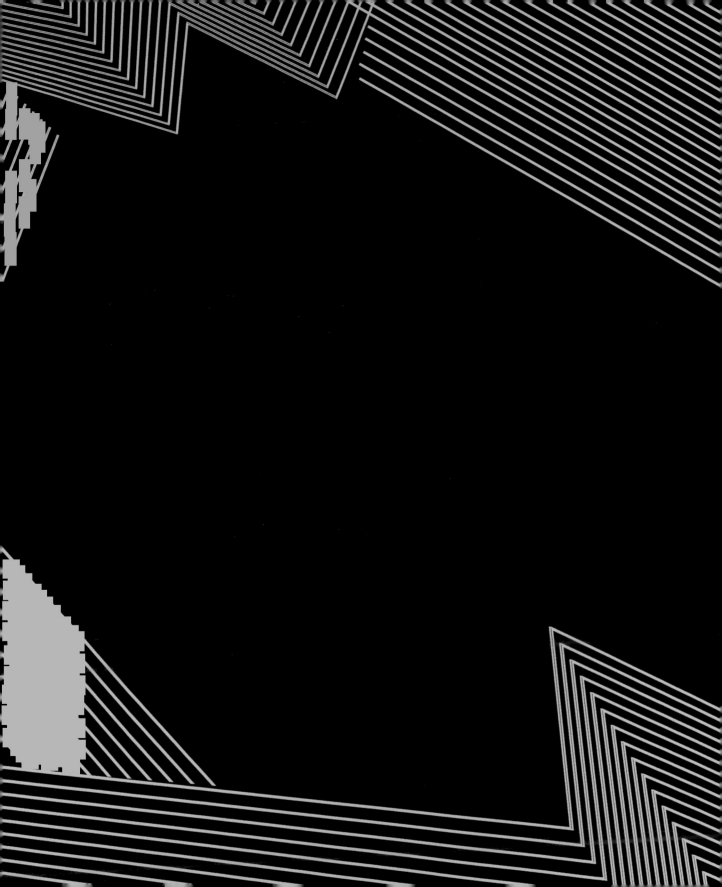

# RESTLESS ARTISTS

**If the first artists you think of are white men from Europe,
you'll be blown away by these five women whose talent with
a paintbrush, a pen, or a pirouette was simply breathtaking.**

Close your eyes and conjure up an image of the great artists of the past. Who comes to mind? Picasso? Rembrandt? Michelangelo, maybe? What about da Vinci, van Gogh, or Andy Warhol?

We probably don't need to explain what all these Great Artists of History have in common, but we are going to anyway: They're white, they're male, and they're of European descent. Whether or not you've taken an art history class, the names of men like Monet, Renoir, or Degas are ingrained in our collective consciousness as capital *A* artists. Artists to imitate, to idolize, to worship. We suspect that it would take just a little longer for most people to come up with a list of comparable length and breadth of great female artists from history. Sadly, things aren't much better even when we reflect on other forms of "high culture," such as literature and classical music. How many female composers can you name?

Art is more than the physical canvas from which a portrait stares back at you. It is greater than the musical notes on a page, more than the accumulation of pages of a novel, and stronger than the marble of a statue. Art, in all its many forms, is a historical and cultural treasure. We cherish it for the ways it memorializes, entertains, challenges, imagines, and subverts. The value of art is so widely understood that when precious works are in danger of loss or destruction, folks risk their lives to preserve them.

Our cultural values aren't just passed down to us through politics or formal education. No matter how we define it, art permeates every aspect of our lives. It is one of the ways we learn about ourselves and others. Through art, we are constantly forming and shaping our cultural understanding of the world.

So, it's pretty tragic that white men from the West continue to occupy an outsized place in our global imagination. By making them the bearers and representatives of culture, we essentially allow them to make society in their image. But what about everyone else? Where are the women?

The reality is that women have been creating art in one form or another since humans began to walk on this planet, but their works have rarely been acknowledged. Women have traditionally been excluded from producing many forms of high art, and their creative work is often dismissed as not being real art at all. Women's work in the domestic realm—cooking, sewing, knitting—is thought of as labor, not art, no matter how exceptional. Things are slowly changing, but think about it: For many people a great female cook is still a cook, while a great male cook is a chef. It's no surprise that with greater respect comes greater cultural, social, and often economic benefits. Meanwhile, women's creative work continues to be overlooked.

The following selection of female artists were pioneering, transcendent, and uncompromising in fields as diverse as film, dance, literature, and fine arts. They demonstrated breathtaking talent and determination in the face of what was often appalling opposition from their families, governments, or competing artists. And yet, despite their achievements, many of them have quietly faded from our memory. It's high time that we recover their names and legacies. May the lives and works of these restless women inspire you to seek out today's great female artists and help amplify their visions.

## ELEVENTH CENTURY

# MURASAKI SHIKIBU

## A LIFE IN INK

If you've ever fallen in love with a novel, you know the moment: You look at the clock, it's one in the morning, and you still can't put the book down. You've been pulled into a world conjured by someone else's imagination, where the thoughts and feelings of the people on the page are as real as your own.

It's hard to imagine a time before novels existed, but there was, in fact, a first novel. And if we want to understand how it came into being, we have to look more than a thousand years into the past, at the writing desk of one woman.

Her name was Murasaki Shikibu, or at least that's the only name we can give her now. Born into an aristocratic Japanese family sometime in the 970s, she lived at a time when the names of women, even notable ones, were rarely recorded. *Murasaki* comes from the tale she created, and *Shikibu* refers to a position her father once held.

Murasaki lived in an intensely cloistered world where women were constantly shielded from public view by screens or curtains. Sometimes it was easier to identify an aristocratic woman by the distinctive pattern of a protruding sleeve than by her face. Yet despite the often-suffocating limitations on their lives, women like Murasaki were educated and expected to be highly literate.

The granddaughter of a famous poet and the daughter of a scholar, Murasaki became conversant in Japanese and Chinese

literature so quickly that she was considered something of a literary prodigy. In her diary, Murasaki recorded her father's reaction when he realized exactly how talented she was: "Just my luck! What a pity she was not born a man!"[19]

In her early twenties, Murasaki married a man old enough to be her father, who died only two years after their marriage but not before they had a daughter. Instead of marrying again, the gifted young widow began work on *The Tale of Genji*, an intricate saga of romance and intrigue in the life of an imperial prince.

*The Tale of Genji* is often considered the first modern novel because Murasaki offered readers not just a chronicle of events, but deep psychological insight into the characters and their inner lives. Her story made history because it was more than just a story: It was a complex literary portrait of what it means to be human.

Although the hero of *The Tale of Genji* is a man, Prince Genji, Murasaki filled her novel with multifaceted female characters who provided a rare glimpse into how it felt to be a woman in her world. As Virginia Woolf later wrote, when Murasaki set out to illuminate the complicated life of the prince, she "naturally chose the medium of other women's minds."[20]

*The Tale of Genji* earned Murasaki a permanent place in literary history. It may also have helped her secure a position at the Imperial Court, where she became an attendant and occasional tutor to Empress Jōtō Mon'in. Murasaki became quite close with the empress and even secretly taught her Chinese—a language only men were supposed to learn.

Although it was a comfortable life, Murasaki was often lonely, and her literary fame made her the target of court gossips, who called her pretentious, arrogant, and unfriendly—complaints often heard about successful women even today.

No one is sure exactly when Murasaki died, but the legacy she left behind changed Japanese literature forever and left a mark on the broader world of fiction that can never be erased. Throughout history, "great novels" have traditionally been considered the domain of male writers, while tales of romance—especially those written by women—are often dismissed as frivolous or inferior.

But history itself tells a very different story. Not only was the first novel a romance, but it was one of the greatest literary masterpieces in human history, and it was written by a woman. Because she dared to imagine the world in ways that no one had before, we can still hear her voice echoing through time more than a thousand years later, daring us to imagine worlds of our own.

# ARTEMISIA GENTILESCHI
## THE BRUSH AND THE SWORD

To know seventeenth-century Italian painter Artemisia Gentileschi, you must seek her in the shaded canvas. If you surrender to the epic grandeur of the Baroque style, with its half-light, vivid hues, and richly rendered textures, you will find her there, alongside the fearless, avenging female subjects who dominate her work and speak to us across time and distance. Renaissance master Artemisia Gentileschi lived a life as full of operatic tragedy and dizzying drama as any of the women she painted, and through them, she made a forceful statement about the enduring power of female resilience, using only the language of pigments and oil paints, turpentine and brushes.

Born in 1593 to a mother who died when Artemisia was only twelve, the young girl was taken in hand by her father, Orazio, a celebrated painter in his own right. At seventeen, Gentileschi completed one of her most enduring works, *Susanna and the Elders*. The subject, like many that she would wrestle with throughout her career, came from the Bible: It is the story of the virtuous Hebrew woman Susanna, who is beset by the harassing attentions of two powerful men. Susanna refuses their attentions, and they accuse her of having sex with another man. Her virtue—and by extension, her life—is put on trial. The painting was so powerful, assured, and mature that for many years

# "A WOMAN'S NAME CAUSES DOUBT UNTIL HER WORK IS SEEN."

some sources insisted that her father must have painted it.

Orazio Gentileschi was determined to nurture the precocious talent of his daughter, and he hired tutor after tutor to refine her skills. One such tutor was Agostino Tassi, a man who had been welcomed into the Gentileschi home when Artemisia was seventeen to assist her with learning perspective, a crucial skill for any painter.

What Tassi did, however, was cruelly hound Gentileschi day after day and force himself on her. The violation was devastating. Though she was in no way responsible, Gentileschi believed implicitly that her virtue had been destroyed and that she had been "ruined." Tassi issued oily promises to marry her, and as unfathomable as it may sound, they must have seemed like a lifeline to the poor girl. In the deeply conservative society in which Artemisia Gentileschi lived, marrying her attacker would have salvaged her honor. Knowing that she was traumatized by the physical and emotional harm he had done to her, Tassi dangled the promise of their marriage before Artemisia to force her consent to repeated encounters.

Ultimately, however, Orazio Gentileschi learned of Tassi's crimes, and his wrath was stirred. He demanded that Tassi be charged with rape and pressured the courts until Tassi stood trial. The proceedings were infamous. The records of this notorious event are some of the earliest historical evidence of rape trials in Europe. Sadly, Artemisia's treatment at the hands of the magistrates was little better than her molestation by Agostino Tassi. Tassi was allowed to make wild, unfounded accusations about Artemisia's virtue in the courtroom, sometimes making up such ludicrous claims about her promiscuity that he even contradicted himself. And yet, despite the grotesque spectacle he presented, it is Artemisia who was forced to prove her honesty. In the face of Tassi's counteraccusations, Artemisia had to endure cords pulled constantly tighter around her fingers while repeatedly swearing her testimony was true.[21] Her hands—her painter's hands—were brutalized, and yet she never recanted her testimony. Tassi was eventually convicted, but it appears he served little jail time, if any. He died poor, and his name has been largely forgotten, as it should be.

But the specter of those devastating experiences hung over the rest of Artemisia's life and inform how we view much of her art today. Take her four paintings of Judith and Holofernes. Like the biblical Susanna, Judith was a virtuous Hebrew woman. Unlike Susanna, Judith is her own avenging angel. An Assyrian general, Holofernes, has besieged Judith's people. Determined to act, Judith charms her way into the Assyrian camp and uses Holofernes's sexual desire for her to enter his tent, where she beheads him. Critics have long pointed to Gentileschi's repeated depictions of the resolute Judith as evidence of her rage and frustration—and her emphatic refusal to be made a victim. Her Judiths are fearless, and they grasp both Holofernes's head and their bloody swords with determination.

In an arranged marriage soon after the trial, Gentileschi wed another artist and moved to Florence, where it must have been slightly easier to escape the notoriety. She continued to work and develop her style, and within four years, when she was only twenty-three, she was made a member of Florence's prestigious Academy of Design— a notable achievement for both her age and her gender, as she was the first woman ever admitted.

Despite enjoying the patronage of Grand Duke Cosimo II de' Medici, Gentileschi suffered in her personal life. She bore four children in five years, only one of which survived, and she and her husband ran up debts before they parted ways in 1623. Nevertheless, her paintings continued to win praise, and her network of patrons grew, even if they didn't always pay what she was worth. Ever one to stand up for herself, Gentileschi refused to be cowed. In correspondence that still exists, she diplomatically but firmly pushes back against men who tried to denigrate her talent. In a letter to patron Don Antonio Ruffo, for instance, she slyly commiserates, "I sympathize greatly with your Lordship, because a woman's name causes doubt until her work is seen."[22]

During this period, she trained her daughter, Palmira, as a painter while continuing to produce masterpiece after masterpiece herself. She was celebrated in her own time, and then gradually, like a canvas hidden in the attic, she faded from our memory. It is inarguable that her talent rivaled Baroque masters such as Caravaggio, but Caravaggio's name—like Rembrandt or Leonardo da Vinci—has traveled down to us through time. Artemisia Gentileschi is little known outside of art history circles, although a comparatively large number of her works still exist. It is only in the last half century that her reputation, like her art, has been brought back into the light, where it belongs.

# TWENTIETH CENTURY

## THROUGH THE LENS

Whether you're a hard-core film history buff or just an armchair enthusiast who likes curling up with a bowl of popcorn and a movie on Saturday night, you can probably name at least a handful of important directors. And regardless of genre, era, or budget, we'd be willing to bet that most of the names that spring to mind most quickly belong to men. Women have been an integral part of the myth, magic, and medium of filmmaking since the dawn of the silent film era. And while we remember the expressive faces and bobbed hair of several early film stars who charmed us in front of the camera, we have very little memory of the brilliant women who worked behind it. Female writers and directors weren't nearly as rare in early filmmaking as we might imagine. It's estimated that between 1911 and 1925 half of all screenplays were written by women.

One of the women whose work has been unjustifiably forgotten is Lois Weber, the first woman inducted into the Motion Picture Directors Association. Weber was a prolific auteur who wrote and directed more than forty feature films and an untold number of shorts over a twenty-five-year career in cinema. She also starred in quite a few, too!

In the summer of 1879, Florence Lois Weber was born in Allegheny, Pennsylvania, to George and Tillie Weber. A middle child between two sisters, Weber was always writing and making up stories, and her

# "CERTAINLY I'VE WRITTEN AND PUBLISHED STORIES EVER SINCE I COULD SPELL AT ALL."

father, an upholsterer and decorator, encouraged her creativity. Weber couldn't recall a time when she wasn't writing: "Certainly I've written and published stories ever since I could spell at all."[23]

By the time Weber entered the film industry in her early twenties, she had already dabbled in several different careers. She spent time as a touring concert pianist and a kindergarten teacher in Pittsburgh before heading off to New York to pursue a career in light opera. It didn't work out, and she returned to Allegheny when her father fell ill. An uncle in Chicago, however, connected her with a musical theater group, and she toured with them before joining a production of *Why Girls Leave Home*. There she met stage manager Phillips

Smalley, and their whirlwind romance was fit for the big screen: It's reported that they were engaged a day after meeting and were married a few months later.

Smalley continued to work in theater while Weber traveled with him and wrote stories. Eventually some of her stories sold, and she decided to try out film. During its infancy, film as an art form was considered pretty lowbrow, especially compared with theater. But Smalley left his stage career to follow his wife's film pursuits.

In the fall of 1910, Weber and her husband joined Rex Motion Picture Company in New York. Weber was an unstoppable creative machine: For over three years, she wrote one "scenario" (an early industry term for a short film) a week, while also directing and even starring in many of them. Critics and audiences alike celebrated these films for their high quality and interesting subject matter. Weber noted, "No amount of clever acting can redeem a character poorly drawn, or a play that is hopelessly deficient in plot and execution."[24] She was constantly arguing for better and more nuanced filmmaking, emphasizing the importance of character development. Frustratingly, we're still wrestling with some of the same concerns that bothered Weber over a century ago: poor characterization and flat writing—particularly when it comes to women in film.

Weber's work consistently centered on female characters. Unlike some of her contemporaries, she didn't believe that film should be apolitical. Instead, she advocated for film to be a "living newspaper." She was not afraid of controversial topics and wanted to provoke debate and discussion. Her films addressed sexual violence, workplace harassment, birth control, capital punishment, and poverty.

In 1912, Rex Motion Pictures and three other independent companies merged to form the Universal Film Manufacturing Company and expanded operations to Los Angeles. Weber and Smalley packed up and moved west. The pair now had the entire arsenal of Universal available to them. They continued creating and producing weekly scenarios and were able to get more creative with the shooting and filmmaking. Weber and Smalley were always promoted together as a team. They both acted in many of their films, although it was really Weber who did the bulk of the creative work. Smalley acknowledged that regularly, referring to their films as "Mrs. Smalley's pictures." On the Universal lot, Lois commanded respect. She was even appointed mayor of Universal City!

By 1914, Weber was itching to move beyond short films and into creating more feature-length works. She and Smalley left

"NO AMOUNT OF CLEVER ACTING CAN REDEEM A CHARACTER POORLY DRAWN, OR A PLAY THAT IS HOPELESSLY DEFICIENT IN PLOT AND EXECUTION."

THE *LOS ANGELES TIMES* WROTE, "WITHOUT A DOUBT ONE OF THE BIGGEST AND MOST OUTSPOKEN, YET ARTISTIC PRODUCTIONS YET SEEN ON A LOCAL SCREEN."

Universal for Bosworth Inc., and it was there in 1915 that Weber created the film that would really make her mark on the industry, *Hypocrites*.

A film about a monk showing people their hypocrisy, *Hypocrites* was a critical and financial success, earning over $133,000 ($3.2 million in 2017)—more than seven times its production budget. Critics praised it for elevating the medium of film into a serious art form. *Variety* said, "No one else has attempted as much or has gone as far," and the *Los Angeles Times* wrote, "Without a doubt one of the biggest and most outspoken, yet artistic productions yet seen on a local screen."[25]

Not all reactions to the film were so positive, however. *Hypocrites* inspired a lot of controversy and was banned from several cities on moral grounds. The character Naked Truth is an allegory for . . . well, truth, and the woman who played her wore a flesh-toned bodysuit to appear naked. This was a bit much for censors of the day, and some film historians suggest that when the National Board of Review of Motion Pictures banned female nudity on screen in 1917, it was likely because of *Hypocrites*.

While Weber was quite modern and progressive in some areas, she was nevertheless a product of her time in many others. Her background as a white, middle-class woman is evident in her films, and not all the boundaries she pushed were worthy ones. In one film, she plays a "native" woman; in others, the villains are dark skinned or "foreign" looking. One of her films was even banned in Chicago for anti-Jewish sentiments.

Weber briefly returned to Universal, where she made a series of successful films on social issues of the day. In 1917, she left again, to start her own studio. By the time Lois Weber Productions closed four years later, she had released fourteen features. These films really focused on marriage and domestic life, bringing the private sphere onto the public screen. Sadly, about the time her company shuttered, Weber and Smalley divorced.

Once again, Weber headed back to Universal. This time, however, things weren't quite so bright. Some people suggest that Weber struggled without Smalley as her partner. Although she was fully capable of directing and writing films without him, she did miss his emotional support and inspiration as her muse. The reality may be that Weber's reduced output after her divorce had less to do with not having a man than it did with shifting life circumstances, and the inevitable grief over such a loss, as well as the industry itself starting to transform in the 1920s. Alice Williamson, an English writer proclaimed, "She lost faith in herself and so she lost interest in herself."[26]

Weber's work in the industry had always been distinguished by transition and change, but in the sunset of her career, she was no longer able to move from triumph to triumph. She remarried in 1926, but she and her husband later separated. Although she continued to work at Universal, a studio she helped put on the map, she lacked the kind of working relationships and freedom she once enjoyed, and her few films were not the critical and popular successes they had been. For a while, she assumed an executive role at Universal, heading up its story department and finding new talent.

Weber wasn't the only one to experience this lessening of influence. As the 1920s progressed, women in all sectors of motion pictures—many of whom Weber had worked to support—were being pushed out of the industry they helped establish.

By the time Lois Weber died of a bleeding ulcer on November 13, 1939, her passing merited only a blip in the film press. She had gone from being "recognized as one of the most eminent filmmakers in the industry . . . accorded top salaries, lucrative contracts, hyperbolic press coverage, and enormous creative freedom,"[27] to virtual anonymity. Not only do few people know her name today, but she was largely forgotten in her own lifetime. Less than fifteen years after she took the film world by storm with her tour de force, *Hypocrites*, Weber had grown completely disillusioned. Anthony Slide notes in his book *The Silent Feminists: America's First Women Directors*, that when Weber was asked what advice she'd give to women who wanted to be directors, her response was simple: "Don't try it."[28]

Ouch.

# MARIA TALLCHIEF

## FIREBIRD RISING

What can one say when faced with the closest to
perfection that dancing mortals can achieve?
—Walter Terry in *Bird of Fire*

To witness a dancer at the peak of their talent, moving in sublime rhythm to the music, is to be in the presence of the divine. There is no beauty like the beauty of a dancer's body communicating through movement. It transcends the physical to connect abstract ideas with an audience: the universality of beauty, spirit, and yearning. Dance has been called "the silent language," for it speaks to us without making a single sound.

One driven woman mastered the silent language of ballet and changed the face and soul of dance forever. Nearly five hundred years after ballet was first developed in Italy as entertainment by and for aristocrats during the Renaissance, an Indigenous American dance prodigy took the world by storm with her virtuosity and beauty. Her name was Maria Tallchief, and she was the first American dancer to achieve the prestigious title prima ballerina.

Maria Tallchief was born January 24, 1925, as Elizabeth Marie Tall Chief in Fairfax, Oklahoma, and spent her early years on the Osage Indian Reservation. Her father, Alexander Joseph Tall Chief, was a member of the Osage Nation, and her mother, Ruth Porter, was Scotch-Irish from Kansas. They called their daughter Betty Marie and enrolled her at age three in piano and dance lessons. The little girl showed incredible artistic skill, quickly demonstrating her perfect pitch when she tried to get out of practice by memorizing a tune and playing it by ear. Her mother hoped that Betty Marie would become a concert pianist. Her younger sister, Marjorie, joined her in the lessons when she was old enough.

The girls' mother believed that Fairfax could not provide sufficient support for her children's artistic and educational growth, so when Betty Marie was around eight years old, the Tall Chiefs relocated to Los Angeles. They settled in Beverly Hills, and Betty Marie and Marjorie attended public school. There Betty Marie became the target of racist comments and taunts from her peers about her Native American last name, prompting her eventually to change the spelling to one word.

The sisters were enrolled in piano and ballet classes again, but their new dance instructor was appalled at the lessons they had received in Oklahoma and told them to forget everything they had learned. They needed to restart from the beginning with fundamentals. This could have been discouraging and deflating, but Betty Marie excelled. She and Marjorie performed acts around Los Angeles together, including occasionally with the Los Angeles Civic Opera Company. Unfortunately, their mother was persuaded to allow the girls do a routine rooted in deeply racist and stereotypical caricatures of Indians that Betty Marie, even as a child, felt was inauthentic and troubling. They performed this routine several times, quitting only when they grew too big for the costumes.

Although her mother pushed her toward piano, Betty Marie's heart was set on ballet. She reveled in the tedious repetition of practice and even insisted her parents install a ballet barre in their home. Through endless training, she perfected fouettés, a whipping movement of the leg executed on pointe (this particular technique would get her early recognition on the stage). Betty Marie's raw talent was apparent to teachers and dance scouts alike, and before she finished high school, she was offered a chance to train with the touring Ballet Russe de Monte Carlo. Family pressure kept Betty Marie in school, but after graduation, her plans to attend college evaporated; she followed her dance instructors to New York, and her life as a professional dancer truly began.

From the beginning, however, this life proved to be more difficult than Tallchief anticipated. Sergei Denham, who had offered her the chance with the Ballet Russe, was too busy to see her once she was available. But the drive and determination that had kept Tallchief at the barre in her home, performing fouetté after fouetté until her muscles were beyond exhaustion, would not let her accept Denham's refusal. The endlessly resilient young dancer called the company every day until he spoke to her.

Tallchief was by no means the only American dancer subject to the mercurial whims of ballet directors and patrons. Back then, American dancers were still largely considered inferior to the exemplars of the Russian stage. But as luck would have it, when Tallchief was trying to get an audition with Denham's prestigious company, the Ballet Russe was dealing with a thorny problem. It was 1942. World War II was raging. Russian dancers in the United States were stranded without passports. If they left the country on a tour, they wouldn't be allowed to reenter. This created a vacuum that could only be filled by American dancers.

This unfortunate circumstance gave opportunities to rising dancers who might not have had them otherwise. Tallchief was

## THROUGH ENDLESS TRAINING, SHE PERFECTED FOUETTÉS, A WHIPPING MOVEMENT OF THE LEG EXECUTED ON POINTE.

accepted into the corps of dancers for the Ballet Russe's Canadian tour with no pay and the promise of a bonus if her work was "satisfactory." She grabbed the opportunity and focused so completely on her work that the other dancers thought she was a snob. They'd call her Princess Iceberg and Wooden Indian. It also didn't help that even though Tallchief was the most junior member of the corps, she would occasionally be assigned solos, which is how she received glowing reviews for those difficult fouettés. After their Canadian tour, the Ballet Russe returned to New York and gave Tallchief a salaried position in the corps. Still, because American ballet dancers were looked down

# "SHE WENT THROUGH HER APPRENTICESHIP LOOKING COOL AND COMPOSED WHILE INWARDLY SORE AND ACHING."

upon by audiences, she was encouraged to take a Russian-sounding stage name. So Betty Marie became Maria, but she resisted pressure to change her last name to the Russian-sounding Tallchieva—a rare moment of defiance in an otherwise almost masochistic life of trying to please others.

Tallchief was nearly machinelike in her commitment to her artistic growth. Her resilience came from a deep fear of failing her mother and her teachers. She used dance to distract from her hurt and loneliness, or maybe those difficult feelings fueled her commitment. "Her chin was carried an inch or so higher than was necessary," biographer Olga Maynard wrote. "She went through her apprenticeship looking cool and composed while inwardly sore and aching."[29]

Tallchief worked with some of the most iconic names in ballet, but her partnership with Russian choreographer George Balanchine has loomed largest in her career. Their fiery collaboration brought them both notoriety and fame and gained Balanchine a reputation as "the father of American ballet." The two were wed in 1946, much to the displeasure of Tallchief's family, who were unhappy about the relationship between the previously married, forty-two-year-old Balanchine and his twenty-one-year-old protégé.

In Tallchief, Balanchine found a muse who could master his most ambitious choreography and push herself beyond what was believed possible. The choreography of Balanchine's ballets challenged conventional European and Russian wisdom and demanded a whole new type of performance and a dancer who could execute his daring vision. Tallchief was that dancer. By 1949, she was dancing full-time with Balanchine's New York City Ballet, and he was creating roles specifically for her style and "frightening technical range."

When she was twenty-four years old, Tallchief's years of singularly focused dedication and perseverance reached their culmination in her performance of Balanchine's *Firebird*, whose punishing physical demands pushed the dancer further than it was believed possible. Her triumphant performance in the title role captivated audiences so thoroughly that the usually dignified ovations of the opera house sounded more like stadium roars. With this, Tallchief cemented her place in ballet history.

When asked about her technical feats, Tallchief said, "You do what you have to do, and when you must, then you do a little more."[30]

Tallchief and Balanchine annulled their marriage in 1952. Tallchief's career ebbed and soared through the 1950s and '60s. While she officially remained with the New York City Ballet, she performed with other companies, eventually working with all three major American companies. Her personal life outside of dance was rocky. Soon after separating from Balanchine, Tallchief married a pilot whom she divorced only

two years later for a variety of reasons, including his hot temper. She married Henry "Buzz" Paschen Jr. in 1956, and they had a daughter, Elise Maria Paschen, in January 1959. Buzz loved the theater and ballet, but he hoped that Maria would eventually devote more time to being a wife and mother. Tallchief continued performing throughout the world to incredible reviews, becoming one of the most famous and highest-paid ballerinas, until she retired from performance in 1965 and began to teach. Tallchief settled down with Buzz and Elise in Chicago, where she founded the Chicago City Ballet.

During her career, Maria Tallchief won accolade after accolade, both inside and outside the dance world. Her home state of Oklahoma named June 29, 1953, Maria Tallchief Day. The Osage Tribal Council honored her with the new name Princess Wa-Xthe-Thonba, recognizing her two roles

## "YOU DO WHAT YOU HAVE TO DO, AND WHEN YOU MUST, THEN YOU DO A LITTLE MORE."

# "I WANTED TO BE APPRECIATED AS A PRIMA BALLERINA WHO HAPPENED TO BE NATIVE AMERICAN, NEVER AS SOMEONE WHO WAS AN AMERICAN INDIAN BALLERINA."

as a ballerina in the wider world and a daughter of the Osage people.

Tallchief had a complicated public relationship with her native background. At the height of her fame, Native American associations begged her to act as a spokesperson, but she declined. "I wanted to be appreciated as a prima ballerina who happened to be a Native American, never as someone who was an American Indian ballerina," she writes in her autobiography.[31] It's entirely possible that she was wary of drawing attention to an aspect of her identity that had been weaponized against her in the past. Tallchief rarely publicly discussed racism as an impediment in her life, but in her autobiography, she shares some moments

etched in her memory. Such as when George Balanchine, about to meet her paternal grandmother, said that he felt like John Smith married to Pocahontas. Or when after a performance in Paris, French newspapers referred to her as a redskin. Later in life, Tallchief connected more deeply with her Osage ancestry, working directly with indigenous groups. In her autobiography she writes, "Over the years my Indian roots had acquired deeper meaning for me and became a more prominent part of my public persona."[32]

True artistry from the outside often appears flawless, natural, and utterly effortless, but that is hardly ever the case. Maria Tallchief exercised almost superhuman will to overcome the prejudice of midcentury dance audiences, racist social expectations, and the limits of the human body itself to receive her due on the world stage as a prima ballerina. For her, ballet wasn't simply art, nor simply a job; it was the ultimate expression of who she was and what she could share with the world, and throughout her life, she never stopped striving for perfection.

> I have always wanted my art to service my people—to reflect us,
> to relate to us, to stimulate us, to make us aware of our potential.
> —ELIZABETH CATLETT

The lines that trace the presence of the African diaspora across the globe are sinuous and curved. The stories told by black and brown peoples everywhere, and the images we evoke in our minds, germinated in an African soil but took root in the soil of many other lands. Elizabeth Catlett, printmaker, sculptor, and muralist, worked for over seventy years creating art that evoked the past and present of black experience, often including pre-Columbian and Mexican influences.

Born in 1915 in Washington, DC, to a truant officer mother and mathematics professor father who died before her birth, Elizabeth Alice Catlett chased a dream of artistic freedom, starting at Howard University and continuing through her graduate work at the University of Iowa, where she received the school's first master's degree in sculpture in 1940. Famed painter Grant Wood mentored her at Iowa, encouraging her to produce work from her own personal experience as a black woman. Part of that experience was segregation. Howard had not been her first choice for college. She had

**CATLETT DID NOT ALLOW ANYTHING TO STAND IN HER WAY WHEN IT CAME TO ARTISTIC EXPRESSION. SHE WAS RELENTLESS IN THE PURSUIT OF CREATIVE FREEDOM, EVEN IF IT MEANT LEAVING THE COUNTRY OF HER BIRTH.**

won a scholarship to the Carnegie Institute of Technology, but she was denied entry after the prestigious school learned her race.

After the University of Iowa, Catlett moved to New Orleans and became chair of the Art Department at Dillard University. Not content to allow her black students to remain isolated from the larger currents in the art world, Catlett wanted to expose them to Pablo Picasso's work at an exhibit at the Delgado Museum of Art. The museum did not allow black patrons, so Catlett negotiated to take her students on a Sunday, when the museum was otherwise closed.

Catlett did not allow anything to stand in her way when it came to artistic expression. She was relentless in the pursuit of creative freedom, even if it meant leaving the country of her birth and seeking more appropriate outlets elsewhere. In 1946,

Catlett received a fellowship from the Julius Rosenwald Fund to create new and compelling works celebrating black women via prints, painting, and sculptures. The money enabled Catlett to travel to Mexico, a country that would become her adopted home. It is there that she truly came into her own as part of a progressive community of artists at the printmaking workshop Taller de Gráfica Popular, where they used their art to advance social justice.

Traditional biographies of Catlett spend time discussing her divorce from her first husband, fellow artist Charles White, and her marriage in Mexico to her second husband, Francisco Mora, which is important only insofar as it illustrates the depth to which Catlett embraced her new home. She became the first female professor of sculpture, then head of the department, at the National Autonomous University of Mexico's school of art.

As part of Taller de Gráfica Popular, Catlett embraced populist politics even more deeply. She was investigated by the House Un-American Activities Committee during the 1950s and arrested during a 1958 railroad workers' strike in Mexico City. By the end of the decade, Catlett was facing increasing criticism and pressure from the US Embassy in Mexico for her

## CATLETT'S REPUTATION AS A POWERFUL AND EVOCATIVE ARTIST HAD GROWN. AND YET, BECAUSE HER WORK FOCUSED PRIMARILY ON THE POOR, OR ON BLACK AND BROWN PEOPLE, IT WAS BY NO MEANS UNIVERSALLY ACCEPTED OR UNDERSTOOD.

political activity. But Catlett never lessened her commitment to populism or worker-centered causes. She renounced her American citizenship and became a Mexican citizen. However, Catlett paid a price for her commitment. In 1962, the US State Department formally declared her an "undesirable alien."

But to be a woman in the world, and a black woman at that, is to be no stranger to being unwanted and ostracized. This quality of being an "undesirable alien" is nothing new to a black woman conscious of her place in the world, and rather than recant her past actions or run from them, Catlett worked harder to support the oppressed people of the United States and Mexico through her art. She continued to

raise her family in Mexico and remained a vital part of the community.

She collaborated with activists such as Angela Davis, with whom she organized the Mexican Provisional Committee of Solidarity in 1969. The poster she created through that partnership, *Freedom for Angela Davis*, is typical of her work: socially committed and centered on black women.

By 1971, the US government had relented a bit in its harsh estimation of Catlett and granted her a special visa to enter the country to attend her one-woman exhibition in Harlem. It was her first trip back to the States in ten years. By that point, Catlett's reputation as a powerful and evocative artist had grown. And yet, because her work focused primarily on the poor, or on black and brown people, it was by no means universally accepted or understood. Even today, it is not uncommon for disdainful critics to dismiss her imagery as trite or cliché, and it's hard to believe that the summation isn't at least partially due to her subject matter. Western notions of art's value rest on its conformity to European Renaissance models. Catlett's unwavering focus on black women, for one, pulls her strongly out of that sphere.

The minimizing of Catlett's work by many critics rests partially on the combination

# CATLETT WAS A DESCENDANT OF SLAVES WHO WERE EXPRESSLY FORBIDDEN FROM CREATING ART FOR ART'S SAKE.

of her subject matter with her chosen formats: murals in public spaces; prints, which she chose because of their cheapness, portability, and accessibility; and sculpture, which was heavily indebted to pre-Columbian and West African styles, not classic European ones. Catlett often created powerfully expressive mother-and-child sculptures, but as with many black artists who feature blackness and black identity in their work, hers is often considered niche. It is rarely valued in the same way as work by white male artists who feature whiteness. Another strike against her was that Catlett was less concerned with whether her art was hung in a museum than whether it served the cultural and political needs of the people around her.

Criticism of Catlett's work tends to fall into two main categories. Her early work is often dismissed as "WPA art," and the art of her middle period is often devalued as mere "protest" art. ("WPA art" is often an insult meant to minimize music, literature, or art that was subsidized by the US government through the Works Progress Administration during the 1930s.) Both critiques suggest that Catlett's art is artistically negligible and somehow less "pure" than art that does not have an explicitly political message or whose creator toils in a studio supported by private patrons.

But Catlett was a descendant of slaves who were expressly forbidden from creating art for art's sake. Art had to serve a tangible purpose, and filling a spiritual or cultural need was secondary. There is a direct line from the slaves who were not allowed to carve or paint but who could cast spirit jugs for grave markers to Catlett, who demands that her art be useful, that it speak to the people from whom it sprang. Catlett's connections to the Mexican public art movement and to the Black Power–Black Arts movement ensured her integrity as an artist for and from the community.

# RELENTLESS AMAZONS

When the world told them that they weren't as strong as men,
these six daring dames used their blades, bikes, and bodies
to smash that myth into smithereens.

hen women are allowed to unfurl their wings, we soar. When our arms are not bound, we are fierce warriors. If our feet remain unshackled, we sprint. If our spirits are not suppressed, we explode with energy and lust for life. We can be superheroes.

Of all the ways that women have been denied independence, agency, and self-determination throughout history, one of the saddest is the lack of opportunity to fully live in and through their own bodies. The rules about what is and what isn't considered appropriate for a woman's body feel terrifyingly inescapable. We're beaten down by a deafening symphony of voices that tell us that women are not natural athletes, that women don't want to push their bodies to the limit, that women will always be physically inferior to men.

You know what those voices are really saying? They're telling us to stay small. Small in form and small in spirit.

WOMEN WHO ENGAGE IN HISTORICALLY MASCULINE TYPES OF ACTIVITIES SUCH AS BOXING OR FOOTBALL ARE STILL DERIDED AS "BUTCH" AND THEREFORE LESS DESIRABLE TO MEN—AS IF THAT SHOULD BE WOMEN'S PRIMARY CONCERN.

Compared with the ways that women have been denied access to education, political influence, or financial resources, the fact that women are denied the right to be loud, physically adventurous, or *big* might seem like a small thing. And yet, those rigid demands upon women, young and old, effectively diminish us in more profound ways. It discourages women from more than just playing sports (although that's not a small thing); it subtly teaches us to be demure, quiet, and invisible. When we are busy being demure, quiet, and invisible, we start to believe that we are not destined to be leaders, decision makers, or authorities.

Expectations like these, whether conscious or unconscious, solidify the divisions between what is considered proper "femininity" and proper "masculinity" (and don't even get us started about how that completely erases any concept of gender outside of this rigid binary).

Women are allowed to exercise control over their own bodies in comparatively few ways. Although many women have increasingly made a place for themselves in sports arenas where they have traditionally been unwelcome, many more feel tremendous social pressure to focus their considerable energies in a comparatively limited range of activities. For every female football player, weightlifter, or shot-putter you can name, there are far more young women who have internalized the anxiety that certain forms of physical exertion are not feminine—often because of the fear that physical mastery of those activities requires, or will result in, a more "masculine" form. In the same way, physical activities that do have a sizable female contingent—gymnastics, dance, or ice skating, for instance—often have radically different standards for excellence when men are judged versus when women are judged. Consider a sport like ice skating. Judges at the highest levels prioritize smallness, thinness, or indefinable qualities like gracefulness for female competitors; and those skaters who are more athletic (which often means more adventurous on the ice) are often penalized. When we talk about female athletes or sports figures, how often do we hear the same terms that we use for male sports figures—commanding, dominating, intimidating—and mean it in a purely complimentary way? In fact, the number of female athletes we talk about at all is dwarfed by the numbers of male athletes who are household names.

The fact is, women who engage in historically masculine types of activities such as boxing or football are still derided as "butch" and therefore less desirable to men—as if that should be women's primary concern. When women do participate and succeed in sports traditionally associated with men, they are often still marketed to the general public in a way that emphasizes that they are still beautiful, sexy, or feminine. Western cultures don't know what to do with women who are not packaged in ways meant to be desirable for male audiences. We see this on television in both amateur and professional sports, as well as the array of video games that have been built around major sports franchises like FIFA, the NBA, the NFL. Although the average person can identify some remarkable female athletes or follow them via sports media, coverage of men's sports is still the overwhelming norm. And in some media, like video games, if there are women on the court or on the field, they're much more likely to be cheerleaders than players.

There are serious consequences when women fail to uphold what we consider to be the feminine ideal. When you add race into the mix, things become even more vicious. When the best tennis player in the world, of any gender, is continually mocked for being too muscular, too manly—for

WHEN THE BEST TENNIS PLAYER IN THE WORLD, OF ANY GENDER, IS CONTINUALLY MOCKED FOR BEING TOO MUSCULAR, TOO MANLY—FOR SIMPLY BEING *TOO MUCH* ALTOGETHER—WE KNOW THAT THE ROOT OF THAT MOCKERY LIES IN HER BEING A BLACK WOMAN.

# REAL WOMEN HAVE ALWAYS BEEN PUSHING THEIR BODIES TO THE LIMITS. WE JUST HAVEN'T BEEN PAYING ATTENTION.

simply being *too much* altogether—we know that the root of that mockery lies in her being a black woman. Serena Williams's own body is weaponized against her.

The only time that women are allowed some measure of freedom with regard to their bodies is when they are children. Prepubescent girls are allowed to rough-house, play around with the boys, and reject notions of femininity that they might not be interested in, although some people still refer to these girls with the sexist term tomboys. But as soon as girls start to grow up, they are expected to fall in line.

Interestingly, although we don't carve much space in our cultural imagination for physically dominant women in real life, many of our fables, folktales, and legends are rife with exciting stories about secret societies of strong, imposing women. The version many of us know best comes from Greek mythology: the Amazons. Said to live isolated lives devoted to sport and war,

heedless of the dictates of the outside world, Amazons were fully self-sufficient and completely autonomous. Their bodies, and their lives, were structured to give full rein to female independence. When we call someone an "amazon" today, we mean that she's a towering, aggressive figure.

But we don't need to rely on myth to confirm what we already know. Real women have always been pushing their bodies to the limits. We just haven't been paying attention. In the following section, we explore a tiny fraction of the relentless amazons throughout history who have brushed off critics and jumped into the arena of life: They have struck out baseball greats, ridden the highways of America alone on the back of a motorcycle, and wrestled men into submission. The small-minded people who like to think women are inferior to men and spout out all kinds of ludicrous nonsense to justify the subjugation of women . . . well, we're guessing they've never met women like these.

# THIRTEENTH CENTURY

# KHUTULUN

## THE UNDEFEATED

**O**nce upon a time there was a princess who . . . can you fill in the blanks? We all know these bedtime stories. But imagine the kind of women we'd raise if the bedtime stories we told our children featured more princesses like Khutulun of Mongolia?

Khutulun, whose name comes from Hotol Tsagaan, meaning "all white" in Mongolian, was quite the character. It wasn't entirely unusual to have women skilled in battle during the Mongol Empire of the thirteenth century, but it wasn't precisely common either. But even among the ferocious and robust female warriors of her time, Khutulun definitely sticks out. Born around 1260 to a regional ruler named

Qaidu Khan, Khutulun learned early to race across the steppes on horseback and to use her eagle eye to guide her archer's bow. As the daughter of a minor noble, her skills were put to frequent use: in hunting and defense of her father's lands.

What little Westerners know about the fascinating figure of Khutulun comes from thirteenth-century Italian explorer, writer, and merchant Marco Polo, whose evocative accounts of travels in the "mysterious Orient" are one of the main sources for information on figures from this era and region. Polo paints a stirring picture of Khutulun in battle, one that practically leaps off the page, noting that this warrior princess would "make a dash at the host of

the enemy, and seize some man there out, as deftly as a hawk pounces on a bird, and carry him to her father; and this she did many a time."[33]

But as dashing a figure as Khutulun cut on her rugged steed, the place where she really excelled was wrestling. No man could best her in a wrestling match. Not a single one! Betting on wrestling matches was a common Mongol pastime, and horses were common betting currency. Khutulun never lost.

By the time Khutulun approached the age where marriage and motherhood were in the cards, she had developed a novel way of selecting (or refusing to select, as the case may be) a potential partner: She decreed that only a man who could beat her at wrestling would be worthy of taking her hand in marriage.

The competition began. Challenger after challenger appeared to vie for the resolute princess's hand. Each attempt cost the contender ten horses. One by one, men stepped forward to wrestle Khutulun into wedded bliss. One by one, she dominated them and collected their wagers. And that's how Khutulun ended up with a sea of horses and no husband. According to one story, a very attractive suitor showed up with one thousand horses. Khutulun's mother and father were eager for her to finally settle

AS DASHING A FIGURE AS KHUTULUN CUT ON HER RUGGED STEED, THE PLACE WHERE SHE REALLY EXCELLED WAS WRESTLING. NO MAN COULD BEST HER IN A WRESTLING MATCH.

down. They pleaded with her to throw the match and finally accept a proposal. Khutulun was having none of it. She strode into the wrestling ring with her trademark confidence. She won the match, claimed the thousand horses, and sent the suitor packing.

It's not hard to see why Khutulun's father, Qaidu Khan, cherished the opinions and self-assurance of his fiery daughter over those of her fourteen brothers. She helped her father govern his kingdom and lead his army of forty thousand warriors. Qaidu was the cousin and rival of the infamous Kublai Khan, the grandson of the notorious conqueror Genghis Khan. The armies of Kublai and Qaidu clashed on the battlefield in seemingly perpetual explosions of conflict. And thundering across those battlefields on her sturdy horse with her unstoppable bow was the relentless Khutulun, never leaving her father's side.

## MARRIAGE DIDN'T STOP KHUTULUN FROM PARTICIPATING IN DEVELOPING MILITARY STRATEGY, RUNNING KINGDOM AFFAIRS, AND FIGHTING IN BATTLES ALONGSIDE HER FATHER.

Nobles, even minor ones like Khutulun and her family, were subject to intense scrutiny and fanciful conjecture. The princess's closeness with her father, and her lack of a husband, stirred up gossip. Rumors went around that she was considering a union with her cousin, the ruler of Persia and Mesopotamia, and there was even the vicious and vile suggestion that she was in an incestuous relationship with her father.

It's been suggested that the pernicious nature of this last rumor led to Khutulun finally agreeing to marry. It's difficult to trace exactly what happened, but one story says:

[Khutulun] married Abtakul after he supposedly came to court on a mission to murder her father, Qaidu Khan. When he was captured, his mother offered herself for punishment instead of him, but Abtakul refused his mother's aid.

Supposedly, Qaidu Khan so respected the mother for trying to save the son and respected the son for trying to save the mother, that he took him into his service and commissioned him as an army officer. Later, when Abtakul was wounded in a battle with Khubilai Khan's army, he returned to the royal camp to recuperate. At that point, Khutulun met him for the first time and fell in love with him.[34]

Marriage to her father's would-be assassin didn't stop Khutulun from participating in developing military strategy, running kingdom affairs, and fighting in battles alongside her father. Her dedication to him never wavered. When Qaidu Khan succumbed to dysentery in 1301, he wanted to leave his kingdom in the charge of his devoted daughter, but she refused to become the next khan. Instead, one of her brothers assumed the mantle of leadership, and Khutulun remained in charge of the army. She looked after her father's tomb for the rest of her life.

Khutulun followed her father in death only five years later, and this amazing athlete and warrior passed into history. She was an inimitable model of a princess who carved her own way in the world, undefeated to the end.

# ANA DE URINZA AND EUSTAQUIA DE SONZA

## THE UNSHEATHED SWORDS

Potosí. An Andean city overshadowed by a majestic peak and paved with the bountiful ore from gushing silver mines. A city so rich, so drenched in money, that by the seventeenth century, aristocrats lived like gods among men.

These descendants of Spanish settlers surrounded themselves in luminous luxury. Draping themselves in silks and rich fabrics, they feasted and imbibed, indulging in glittering parties that seemed born of a wonderful dream. It was a rarefied atmosphere of affluence and splendor that beggared the imagination.

But there was another Potosí. Another side to this city that even four hundred years ago bulged with more than 160,000 inhabitants, the largest city in the Americas. *This* Potosí was dangerous and rough, and life was hard. If you were one of the teeming masses of the poor—who vastly outnumbered the wealthy few—then your life was worth almost nothing. You endured a daily fight simply to survive. This Potosí was less like a shining city on a hill and more like a boomtown out of a Wild West movie. Close your eyes and feel the choking dust rising on the wind. Smell the leather shirts that people layered three and four deep to protect themselves from the thief's stabbing blade.

Smell the musky horseflesh as banditos race through the thoroughfares. Listen to the clamor of the tavern brawls spilling into the street and yells of raucous gambling. If you had the stomach for it (and the steel at your side), then this Potosí offered as much excitement as the more refined one in the sun-soaked villas of the rich. You just had to stay alive to enjoy it.

Out of the almost impossibly lurid backdrop of these two Potosís emerged Doña Ana de Urinza and Doña Eustaquia de Sonza, women who became one of the most celebrated duos in Peruvian history. Donning lace and finery by day, then slipping into the clothes of swashbuckling caballeros at night, Urinza and Sonza cut dashing figures through seventeenth-century Potosí and its environs like celluloid heroes from Hollywood's golden age.

Not much is known about Urinza's early life, not even the exact year of her birth. Many believe that, unlike Sonza, she was born poor in the desperate sections of the city. Survival was a daily struggle, and it's likely that the fearlessness, resiliency, and incredible bravery she demonstrated throughout her life were traits gained on the lawless streets of Potosí when she was a small girl.

At some point, Ana met and became fast friends with Eustaquia, whose background

DONNING LACE AND FINERY BY DAY, THEN SLIPPING INTO THE CLOTHES OF SWASH-BUCKLING CABALLEROS AT NIGHT, URINZA AND SONZA CUT DASHING FIGURES THROUGH SEVENTEENTH-CENTURY POTOSÍ AND ITS ENVIRONS LIKE CELLULOID HEROES FROM HOLLYWOOD'S GOLDEN AGE.

and social position were worlds apart from her own. Ana was the leather; Eustaquia was the lace. One was hard as steel, the other was soft as feather down. At least, that's how it should have been—two diametrically opposite girls, who couldn't have been more different. And yet, by the time the girls were twelve, they were so close and so alike that Eustaquia's father adopted Ana into the family and raised her alongside his own daughter so that they could be even closer.

In this era, women of Eustaquia's station were limited to a fairly narrow sphere of activity, and lessons for the girls focused on needlework, dancing, art, and music. But the girls could not resist the allure of Eustaquia's brother's sword-fighting lessons. Creeping through the corridors of the Sonza villa, they

# THEY CONCOCTED A WILD SCHEME AND BEGAN TO SNEAK FROM THE VILLA AT NIGHT, DRESSED AS MEN, THEIR LONG HAIR TUCKED UNDER HATS.

spied on the sword master and mimicked his movements as he demonstrated technique for the boy. Day by day, the two girls grew more fascinated with the art of fencing. Sadly, Eustaquia's brother died young, but rather than dismiss the fencing master, their father allowed Eustaquia and Ana to continue the fencing lessons in the brother's stead. They took to it like birds to air.

Unfortunately, opportunities to use their newfound skills were few and far between for the girls. Rather than let their talents deteriorate, they concocted a wild scheme and began to sneak from the villa at night, dressed as men, their long hair tucked under hats. Thus attired, they made their way through the streets of the city with the kind of assurance that would not have been possible if they presented themselves as two young ladies alone.

But this wasn't a matter of simply playing dress up. Ana and Eustaquia threw themselves into the rough and ready nightlife of Potosí: drinking, gambling, fighting, and flirting with carousing women. They drank up the excitement and adventure of this kind of frontier life, and in the mornings they simply slipped back into their silken gowns and went about their business as young ladies of leisure.

All of this would have been enough to make a fascinating story, but it doesn't stop there. Ana and Eustaquia became something akin to vigilantes on the streets of Potosí. They were fighters in the service of the vulnerable, and their flashing steel swords and loaded muskets were a terror. They fought side by side and never backed down.

In one of the more famous stories told about them, the two girls were set upon by four villainous men. The fight was on. Back to back, Ana and Eustaquia fought. Ana was knocked down, felled by a blow to the head. Eustaquia stood over her friend's body, fought back the men, and prevented them from hurting Ana further. When Ana gradually roused herself, she threw herself back into the fight with such vigor that she nearly severed a man's hand. They dispatched the rest of the scoundrels quickly.

Of course, Ana and Eustaquia could not keep their anonymity forever. It was discovered that they were women under their caballero clothes, and the shocked (but we assume delighted) populace that had been the recipients of their avenging fury began to refer to them as the Valiant Ladies of Potosí. They started to wander further afield, always seeking adventure and excitement. And it wasn't just sword battles and fistfights. Ana, ever the daring one, also got involved in bullfighting. It seemed as if she was afraid of nothing.

When Eustaquia's father died and made the two women his heirs, the sheer number and breadth of their exploits began to lessen. Ana and Eustaquia had to return to Potosí to run the Sonza estate, which was a huge undertaking. Nevertheless, they didn't completely settle down into boring domesticity. They always kept up some hell-raising on the side.

Sadly, the hell-raising eventually claimed a price that was too high for even these high-living ladies to pay. Ana was gored during a bullfight, and the wound never fully healed. She eventually succumbed to her injuries. Eustaquia died only four months later, her heart broken at the loss of her lover and friend.

And so the curtain closed on the swashbuckling, golden adventures of Urinza and Sonza, bringing with it a heartbreaking end to the story of two passionate and gutsy women. Their swords were laid to rest; their capes ceased to fly in the wind; their masks were folded and hidden away. But centuries later, in the stories told about them, these two gallant adventurers still loom larger than life.

THEY WERE FIGHTERS IN THE SERVICE OF THE VULNERABLE, AND THEIR FLASHING STEEL SWORDS AND LOADED MUSKETS WERE A TERROR. THEY FOUGHT SIDE BY SIDE AND NEVER BACKED DOWN.

# WONDER WOMAN

**S**tep right up, ladies and gentlemen! Marvel at the sheer physical magnificence of the mighty and lovely Kati Sandwina, who juggled cannonballs and hoisted grown men above her head without breaking a sweat. A perfect physical specimen, ladies and gentlemen, and proof that the gods do walk among us. Roll up, roll up! Don't miss this opportunity, ladies and gentlemen. Greatness like this doesn't come by just every day!

There is nothing quite so fraught with judgment as a woman's body. Patriarchy defines the ideal body in every era and in every culture, and it is up to individual people to either live up to that ideal or ignore it and pay the price. In our modern era, we often forget that the hyperdisciplined, aggressively slender model of womanhood has not always been something that signaled wealth, health, or class. In many cultures and in many eras, a larger body spoke of a person's access to wealth and leisure and was therefore highly regarded.

It was at the cultural nexus between these two models that we find early twentieth-century strongwoman Kati Sandwina, born Catherine Brumbach in Austria in 1884. Sandwina was the second-oldest child in the huge performing family (fifteen or sixteen children; records are unclear) of Phillipe and Johanna Brumbach, awe-inspiring strength performers in their own right. The giant Phillipe was six-foot-six

# WHEN SHE WAS SIXTEEN, HER FATHER WAS OFFERING 100 MARKS TO ANYONE WHO COULD WRESTLE HER AND WIN. NO ONE COULD.

and had a fifty-six-inch chest. Equally stupendous Johanna sported fifteen-inch biceps. The family traveled all around Europe performing to clamoring crowds.

Kati trained in gymnastics and weightlifting from an incredibly young age to follow her family into the circus arts. It was not long before she was a force to be reckoned with. By the time she was sixteen, her father was offering 100 marks to anyone who could wrestle her and win. No one could.

It was meant to be a fun and thrilling experience for the assembled crowds, and watching this comely young lady completely dominate full-grown men certainly was. But one young man's bout in the ring with Kati would change his life forever. Nineteen-year-old acrobat Max Heymann (shorter and much lighter than Kati) accepted her father's challenge, and although he lost, Kati and Max fell in love. At least, that's the very romantic but very unusual story that became part of their grand history. In any case, two years after they met, they were wed, and they spent the next fifty-two years happily married.

Kati and Max continued to perform around Europe before taking a chance on New York around the turn of the twentieth century. They had very little public profile in America, so in an effort to draw attention, Kati and Max went back to the kind of publicity stunt that had drawn the two of them together. They challenged anyone watching to lift more weight than Kati. No one could! Legend has it that one day, a man named Eugen Sandow, famous the world over as a strongman and fitness model, stepped up to the stage and accepted Kati's challenge. The crowd must have been breathless with anticipation. The two colossi traded off, lifting heavier and heavier weights in turn. Finally, Sandow hoisted a three-hundred-pound weight to his chest. Kati lifted the same weight high above her head. She was the victor.

It's quite likely that the genesis of this extravagant tale owes more than a little bit to Kati and Max billing themselves as "The Sandwinas" when they toured and performed, wowing people across Europe and the East Coast of the United States. They would have been far from the first or last circus strong act to piggyback off Sandow's tremendous fame; doing so was just a savvy marketing move and part of the larger-than-life origin story that Max and Kati, "Europe's Queen of Strength and Beauty," refined over their many years together on the stage.

And yet, for all the acclaim and thunderous applause Sandwina drew from the breathless crowds, she had to fight a never-ending battle to be perceived as feminine. Her costumes, demeanor, and embellished personal history were deliberately crafted to reassure people that she was not in any way manly—even though she could beat men

**FINALLY, SANDOW HOISTED A THREE-HUNDRED-POUND WEIGHT TO HIS CHEST. KATI LIFTED THE SAME WEIGHT HIGH ABOVE HER HEAD. SHE WAS THE VICTOR.**

with what's considered a quintessentially masculine trait: strength. The press at the time took pains to note that Kati was a mother and wife, safely contained by domesticity.

In the 1910s, Sandwina's popularity was at its height. The early part of the twentieth century featured a nasty undercurrent of eugenics propaganda, a pseudoscience concerned with producing a more advanced, "pure" human being, which resulted in racist and classist policies that affected women of color in terrible ways. But for a woman like Kati Sandwina—safely white and European—the cultural obsession with physical perfection translated into wild

## KATI STILL OCCASIONALLY BENT IRON BARS TO THE DELIGHT OF THE BAR'S PATRONS, AND IF ANYONE GOT LIPPY OR OUT OF CONTROL, SHE GAVE THEM THE BUM'S RUSH HERSELF.

popularity. Over her long career, she could pull in as much as $1,500 a week. Everyone wanted a piece of her: Magazines clamored for interviews, and she was even asked to provide motherhood tips. (It was assumed that she could provide vital advice on raising the next generation of super children.)

It was during this period of Sandwina's greatest fame that she leaned into potential controversy by serving as the vice president of the Suffragette Ladies of the Barnum & Bailey Circus. The push toward gaining women the right to vote (which would not happen until 1920 with the ratification of the Nineteenth Amendment) was a contentious issue, and many naysayers criticized the circus performers' participation in the movement as a joke. But as people on the fringe of society, circus performers knew intimately the importance of self-determination, and the female performers took this vital issue very seriously.

By the 1930s, Sandwina's career as a strongwoman was winding down. She was in her late forties—certainly not ancient, but no longer the peak physical specimen she had been twenty years earlier. She and Max worked with the WPA Circus after leaving Barnum & Bailey, but by the next decade, the Sandwinas were ensconced in Queens, New York, as owners of a bar and restaurant. But the bar she stood behind wasn't the only one in her life: Kati still occasionally bent iron bars to the delight of the bar's patrons, and if anyone got lippy or out of control, she gave them the bum's rush herself.

In 1952, Kati Sandwina died of cancer at age sixty-seven. Her exploits and sheer physical dominance were largely forgotten except to bodybuilding historians or seekers of the curious. But such a phenomenal woman deserves to be remembered—not just for what she did on the stage, but what she represented: a real-life Wonder Woman who refused to be made small.

# TWENTIETH CENTURY

# JACKIE MITCHELL

## A LEAGUE OF HER OWN

There's nothing like the smell of roasted peanuts on the late summer air, the crack of a bat hitting a ball, and the exuberant cheers of fans in the stands. Baseball. As American as apple pie and women not getting credit for things that make men uncomfortable.

You've probably heard of Babe Ruth and Lou Gehrig, two of the biggest baseball names of all time. But do you know the name of the seventeen-year-old girl who struck them both out?

So many people react to this story with utter disbelief that decades after it happened, the very idea is still dismissed as a fabrication. But why is it so hard to imagine? Would people have the same reaction if the story involved a talented seventeen-year-old boy?

Jackie Mitchell was the name of this forgotten pitching phenom, and she was born August 29, 1913, to a mother who sold hosiery and a father who worked as an optician. When she was a small child, her parents moved to Memphis, coincidentally into the same building as Dazzy Vance, a minor league pitcher who would go on to lead the National League in strikeouts for seven straight years. Vance worked with the young girl, teaching her how to throw certain pitches, including the "drop ball." This pitch, now called a sinker, goes fast but drops late so that it either ducks under a bat or is hit on the ground, leading to an easy out.

As a teenager, Mitchell attended a baseball training school in Atlanta, where her skills caught the eye of Joe Engel, the president of the Chattanooga Lookouts, a minor league baseball team in Tennessee. Engel would become notorious for all kinds of over-the-top shenanigans to get fans to the games, such as raffling off a house or staging a fake elephant hunt in which men in elephant suits were chased around the field by men in safari outfits. He once traded his shortstop for a twenty-five-pound turkey, which he roasted and served to the press. Another time, he hung fifty cages of canaries around the stadium simply because he liked to listen to songbirds. In 1931, Engel offered Mitchell a contract to play pro ball with the Lookouts, and she accepted.

Mitchell wasn't the first woman to be signed to a professional baseball team. There were all-women teams as early as the 1860s, but they were mostly for show and spectacle, with actors and vaudeville-type performances. However, in 1898, pitcher Lizzie Arlington became the first woman to sign a minor league baseball contract, with the Reading Coal Heavers in Pennsylvania, and to play in a regulation game.

Jackie Mitchell's first (and only) game with the Lookouts took place on April 2,

JACKIE'S MEAN DROP BALL AND ATHLETIC SKILL WEREN'T THE FOCUS OF THE PRESS COVERAGE. INSTEAD, REPORTERS CHOSE TO EMPHASIZE HER FEMININITY. ONE REPORTER WROTE, "THE CURVES WON'T BE ALL ON THE BALL WHEN PRETTY JACKIE MITCHELL TAKES THE MOUND."

1931. The mighty New York Yankees, with the legendary Babe Ruth and Lou Gehrig, were in town for an exhibition. Four thousand eager spectators crowded the stands for the much-hyped event, eager to see a girl pitch to some of the best hitters in the sport. But Jackie's mean drop ball and athletic skill weren't the focus of the press coverage. Instead, reporters chose to emphasize her femininity. One reporter wrote, "The curves won't be all on the ball when pretty Jackie Mitchell takes the mound." Another observed that before she went into her windup "the bobbed hair pitcher pulled out her mirror and powder puff and dusted the shine off her nose."[35]

Chattanooga's manager called the left-handed Jackie to the mound right as Ruth approached the plate.

Here's how it went down:

Jackie throws a drop ball. Ruth lets it go without a swing. . . .

# BALL ONE!

Jackie throws another. Ruth swings and misses. . . .

# STRIKE ONE!

Jackie throws. Ruth swings. . . .

# STRIKE TWO!

At this point Babe Ruth, the Sultan of Swat, gets a little peeved. He even asks for the ball to be inspected.

Jackie. Ruth. . . .

# STRIKE THREE!

Babe Ruth was out!

The Great Bambino threw his bat in anger and left the batter's box. His frustration was not exactly surprising. Just the day before he had told reporters, "I don't know what's going to happen if they begin to let women in baseball. Of course, they will never make good. Why? Because they are too delicate. It would kill them to play ball every day."[36]

Aww, sour grapes, buddy?

But Jackie wasn't done yet. Up next for the Yankees was Lou Gehrig. He was a quieter, more serious player than Ruth, but he was just as dangerous at the plate. On that fateful day, though, the Iron Horse proved no match for Jackie Mitchell and her incredible sinker.

# STRIKE ONE!
# STRIKE TWO!
# STRIKE THREE!

Lou Gehrig was out!

You'd think that would be the beginning of an amazing career for young Jackie, but the story goes that baseball commissioner Kenesaw Mountain Landis heard about her performance against two of baseball's greats and tore up her contract, claiming that baseball was "too strenuous for women." His actions were sad but predictable, given that Landis had a long history of using biological determinism to exclude women and African

## ALTHOUGH JACKIE ROBINSON BROKE THE COLOR BARRIER FOR BLACK MEN IN 1947, WOMEN ARE *STILL* NOT ALLOWED TO PLAY IN THE MAJOR LEAGUES.

American men from the league. These arguments claimed that women and people of color were biologically inferior to white men and therefore shouldn't be afforded the same rights or opportunities. So, y'know, just straight up sexism and racism.

Mitchell was denied the opportunity to wow the crowds in the major leagues, but she couldn't be kept away from the game she loved. She signed with the House of David in 1933, a religious society in Michigan whose founder really liked sports. The House of David had its own baseball team and played other teams in barnstorming tours around the country. Outside of organized baseball, these exhibition games could be almost circuslike in their atmosphere, but they were incredibly diverse. For a long time, this was where women and people of color were "allowed" to play. Although Jackie Robinson broke the color barrier for black men in 1947, women are *still* not allowed to play in the major leagues.

Jackie Mitchell retired from baseball in 1937 and went to work with her father. To this day, the debate still swirls about whether this seventeen-year-old from Memphis really struck out two of the best baseball players of all time. Up until her death in 1987, Jackie swore it was not staged.

We believe her.

Next time someone says you throw like a girl, tear out these pages, hand them over, and say, "Thanks!"

# BESSIE STRINGFIELD

## LEADER OF THE PACK

Revving a powerful engine, racing down a highway with nothing but the blue sky in front of you and the wind at your back—that was the life of the Motorcycle Queen of Miami, Bessie Stringfield, the first black woman to make a solo journey by motorcycle across the United States.

Stringfield was born in 1911 in Kingston, Jamaica, as Betsy Ellis. She lost her mother, a Dutch white woman, when she was an infant, and her black father took her to Boston, where he abandoned her. Orphaned by age five, Betsy was taken in by a wealthy white Irish Catholic family. The religious faith she absorbed there would be a source of strength for the rest of her life. (Stringfield often credited her fearlessness and self-assurance to "the Man Upstairs.") It was in Boston that Betsy first started hankering after motorcycles. She pestered her adoptive mother endlessly for one, finally getting her wish on her sixteenth birthday. "Even though good girls didn't ride motorcycles," Stringfield said.[37] She had no idea how to ride it.

Did that stop her? Not the Motorcycle Queen. She prayed for guidance from the Man Upstairs and put her prayers to paper, then hid them under her pillow. Stringfield said she dreamed that night about shifting gears and operating her new bike, and in the morning, she knew just what to do.

By age nineteen, Bessie was making her way across the country on what she called

# STRINGFIELD SPENT THE WAR DELIVERING VITAL CLASSIFIED MESSAGES ON THE BACK OF HER TRUSTY HARLEY.

"penny tours." She'd flip a penny onto a map and go wherever it landed. She wound up visiting all the lower forty-eight states of America in this way. As if that wasn't enough, she did this when racist Jim Crow laws were still very much in effect in large parts of the country. As a black woman alone on the road, Bessie faced innumerable dangers and untold discrimination. Even something as basic as finding a place to sleep for the night could be a struggle. If she couldn't find a friendly black family willing to share their space, Bessie slept on her bike under gas station lights. She used her jacket as a pillow and put her feet up on the rear fender. Bessie brushed off all these challenges as just part of the territory, even incidents as terrifying as the time she was chased by white supremacists and run off the road.

And yet, Bessie did find a community of good folks on the road. She noted that once

a white gas station attendant let her fill up for free—just because of the sheer novelty of seeing a black female motorcycle rider, let alone one on her own!

By the time the United States was embroiled in World War II, Bessie was in her early thirties, but she wasn't slowing down one bit. Stringfield spent the war delivering vital classified messages on the back of her trusty Harley. Her training involved racing up steep, sandy hills, executing hairpin turns, and making bridges of rope and tree limbs to cross swamps, in case she ever needed to get out of a tight spot.

Although Stringfield had spent time making a living on the carnival circuit with her motorcycle skills, after the war she settled down to a quieter life in Miami, Florida. There, she became a nurse and held that job until she retired. Nevertheless, she kept up her riding, often riding to work or to church on Sunday. Stringfield's boldness on the road earned her the nickname Motorcycle Queen of Miami.

She didn't immediately win over the whole town, though. In the beginning, police officers harassed her, saying black women weren't allowed to ride motorcycles in the city, and she couldn't get a license. Fed up, she went to see Captain Robert Jackson, a white motorcycle officer in Miami's Negro Police Precinct, who asked her to demonstrate her motorcycle skills. Stringfield wowed him with her ability, and he was struck speechless. Eventually they became friends. The police didn't bother her again, and she got her license.

Stringfield also founded a motorcycle club where she enforced a uniform policy that made many men chafe. The uniform was probably meant to present a more palatable image to onlookers of the day. Bikers are by no means fully accepted into mainstream society even today, and in the America of the mid-twentieth century, they were still considered something of an oddity.

Bessie Stringfield was married six times. She kept the name of her third husband after their divorce—at his request. He told her that she had made the name famous. Stringfield had three children during her first marriage, but none of them survived. She had no more. But when thinking about family, she always considered her fellow riders to be the closest, best, most accepting family she could have wished for.

Although she's not well known outside the motorcycle community, Stringfield's legacy among female riders is secure. Through her boldness and self-assurance, she encouraged other women, especially black women, to take to the open road and claim the broad vistas of this country for themselves, not secondhand. Some of those riders honor her today with the annual Bessie Stringfield All Female Ride. It's about family. It's not about being a good girl, but about being yourself. It's about getting out there and riding.

## HER TRAINING INVOLVED RACING UP STEEP, SANDY HILLS, EXECUTING HAIRPIN TURNS, AND MAKING BRIDGES OF ROPE AND TREE LIMBS TO CROSS SWAMPS, IN CASE SHE EVER NEEDED TO GET OUT OF A TIGHT SPOT.

# AFTERWORD

The process of selecting twenty-five (just twenty-five!) stories to present to you in *History vs Women* was complicated, thrilling, frustrating, exciting, worrisome, and inspiring. There are so many women we wanted to include, but the demands of time, resources, and space meant that in the end, brutal choices had to be made. When we think about the amazing rebels, amazons, villains, scholars, and artists that we didn't get to include, we immediately want to start work on volume two.

We tried to remain conscious throughout of our North American, English-language bias as we researched and wrote this book. Although we had the opportunity to learn about hundreds of captivating women, we acknowledge that we were limited to telling the stories of women for whom we could find sources in English (either original or in translation). This represented a real challenge, and we acknowledge that it resulted in a final text that is overwhelmingly weighted toward Western figures. There are rich veins of popular and academic sources from other cultures outside of our own, about truly fascinating historical figures. But unfortunately, our personal limitations meant that we could not investigate or access them in the time we had allotted. As a consequence, there are considerably fewer stories here than we would like about women from sub-Saharan Africa and the global south. Nevertheless, we worked hard to bring you stories of women from as many different backgrounds as we could, and to tell their stories well.

The lack of representation of nonwhite, non-Western women in the media is by no means limited to our project. The reality for many of us is that it is easier to learn about white, Western people than it is to learn about the lives and historical contributions of people of color, queer and trans folks, and people with disabilities. That must change.

We can all do better. Writers, activists, and scholars of feminist history must strive to make our work more inclusive and representative of women around the world, from every nation and ethnic background. They all deserve to have their stories told.

# ACKNOWLEDGMENTS

We are beyond indebted for the love, support, and yes, quiet intimidation, of so many people who helped us create the book you hold in your hands today. Without their encouragement and expert advice, we would have been lost. Our profound thanks go out to Charlie Olsen and William Callahan of Inkwell Management for twisting Anita's arm to make this project happen and for holding our hands through publishing our first book. The entire team at Feiwel and Friends are absolute rock stars who deserve monuments in parks, but we especially want to shout out our editor, Holly West. Her unfailing patience and willingness to answer even the most ridiculous/mundane/simple/basic questions kept our ulcers from multiplying and our anxiety at (nearly) manageable levels. Elizabeth "Starr" Baer, our production editor, never lost her cool over our creative approach to deadlines (although she had every right to), and Morgan Durbin was everything we could have hoped for in a publicist.

We are tremendously grateful to Sherri Schmidt, our rigorous and attentive fact-checker, for the care she demonstrated in her work. Lastly, we want to thank the folks who are most responsible for the actual, physical work of art you are holding in your hands: Kim Waymer, dedicated production manager; April Ward, our phenomenal designer; and our breathtaking artist, T. S. Abe. Her vision and talent were instrumental in making these women come alive on the page.

*History vs Women* was born out of Feminist Frequency's web series *Ordinary Women: Daring to Defy History*. Our deepest thanks to the entire team who worked tirelessly on bringing the stories of these fascinating women to life, especially Elisabeth Aultman, our dynamic producer, and Laura Hudson, our brilliant writer.

On a day-to-day basis, we were lifted up by the generosity and friendship of so many people whose excitement about this book sustained us. Thanks to Jason Porath for his shockingly specific memory about women throughout history, his insightful advice, and invaluable research assistance. His book, *Rejected Princesses*, has been an inspiration to so many. (Go buy it!) And we would be remiss if we didn't send our love to Carolyn Petit and Ashley Ferrell, who picked up the slack when we were deep in the trenches and ensured that Feminist Frequency continued to operate at its peak.

Ebony would like to start by thanking Anita for offering her the opportunity to work side by side on an incredible project like this, but she's still not sure whether Anita was only kidding when she extended the invitation and then got stuck. Ebony sends bear hugs to Francine Crockett, in whose guest room significant portions of this book were written; Kevin Will, who was an inexhaustible fountain of late-night support; and Jennifer Hendrickson, Paul Spencer, and Todd Hudson, who never failed to ask, "Is that book done yet?"

Anita first and foremost wishes to thank Ebony for agreeing to partner on an endeavor as rewarding (and only occasionally stressful) as writing a book. *History vs Women* would not be what it is today without her graceful, lyrical writing and endlessly patient editing skills. Anita thanks her mother, whose relentless perseverance through incredible hardships and ability to dance throughout the night are a constant source of inspiration; and Julia, who always knows the very right thing to say to her when everything feels like chaos. But most of all Anita thanks her cat, Tig, for constantly walking over her research notes and thinking that a laptop is a great resting place.

Lastly, we both want to thank the amazing people who work at the Los Angeles and San Francisco public libraries. Libraries are incredible institutions that we are so fortunate to have access to. Support your public libraries!

## SOURCE NOTES

### RECKLESS REBELS

1. Lorde, *The Cancer Journals*.13.
2. Thomas Hodgkin, *Vietnam: The Revolutionary Path* (New York: St. Martin's, 1981), 22, quoted in Lockard, *Societies, Networks, and Transitions*, 115.

11. Doria Shafik, "Minarets," translated by Afifa Benwahoud, in Ragai and Ragai, doria-shafik.com/.

### REVELATORY SCHOLARS

1925): 53, 80, in Morris, *The World of the Shining Prince*, x.
21. Garrard, *Artemisia Gentileschi*, 453–462.
22. Artemisia Gentileschi to Don Antonio Ruffo, Jan. 30, 1649, in DiCaprio and

Arbaoui, Larbi. "Al Karawiyyin of Fez: The Oldest University in the World." Morocco World News. Oct. 2, 2012. www.moroccoworldnews.com/2012/10/59056/al-karaouin-of-fez-the-oldest-university-in-the-world/.

Badran, Margot. *Feminists, Islam, and Nation: Gender and the Making of Modern Egypt*. Princeton: Princeton University Press, 1995.

Bay, Mia. *To Tell the Truth Freely: The Life of Ida B. Wells*. New York: Hill and Wang, 2010.

Bernardi, Gabriella. *The Unforgotten Sisters: Female Astronomers and Scientists Before Caroline Herschel*. Chichester, UK: Springer Praxis Books, 2016.

Cohen, Marilyn. *No Girls in the Clubhouse: The Exclusion of Women from Baseball*. Jefferson, NC: McFarland, 2009.

Conway-Smith, Erin. "For Margaret Thatcher, Few Tears Shed in South Africa." PRI. April 8, 2013. www.pri.org/stories/2013-04-08/margaret-thatcher-few-tears-shed-south-africa.

Corben, Billy, director. *Cocaine Cowboys 2: Hustlin' with the Godmother*. Documentary film, 97 mins. Rakontur, 2008.

———. "Griselda Blanco: So Long and Thanks for All the Cocaine." Vice. Sept. 4, 2012. www.vice.com/en_us/article/3b5jz8/griselda-blanco-so-long-and-thanks-for-all-the-cocaine.

DiCaprio, Lisa, and Merry E. Wiesner, eds. *Lives and Voices: Sources in European Women's History*. Boston: Houghton Mifflin, 2001.

Donovan, Sandy. *Hypatia: Mathematician, Inventor, and Philosopher*. Minneapolis: Compass Point Books, 2008.

Doster, Adam. "The Myth of Jackie Mitchell, the Girl Who Struck Out Ruth and Gehrig." *The Daily Beast*. May 18, 2013. thebea.st/11Lk79r.

Downey, Kirstin. *Isabella: The Warrior Queen*. New York: Anchor, 2015.

Easley, Annie J. Interview by Sandra Johnson. NASA Headquarters Oral History Project, Johnson Space Center, Aug. 21, 2001. www.jsc.nasa.gov/history/oral_histories/NASA_HQ/Herstory/EasleyAJ/EasleyAJ_8-21-01.htm.

Ernst, Rhys, director. *We've Been Around: Lucy Hicks Anderson*. Documentary short, 5:26. YouTube, June 10, 2016. youtu.be/_DKxsGP9tRY.

Fair, John D. "Kati Sandwina: 'Hercules Can Be a Lady.'" *Iron Game History* 9, no. 2 (Dec. 2005): 4–7.

Ferrar, Ann. "Bessie Stringfield." AMA Motorcycle Hall of Fame, 2002. www.motorcyclemuseum.org/halloffame/.

———. "One Woman's Extraordinary Life on the Road." Bessie Stringfield: Behind Her Authorized Biography (website), 2017. www.annferrar.com/.

Garrard, Mary D. *Artemisia Gentileschi Around 1622: The Shaping and Reshaping of an Artistic Identity*. Berkeley: University of California Press, 2001.

Gosse, Phillip. *History of Piracy*. Mineola, NY: Dover, 2007.

"Great Sikh Women: Mai Bhago." All About Sikhs. (website). www.allaboutsikhs.com/great-sikh-women/mai-bhago.

Harrison, John. "The Sculpture of Elizabeth Catlett." Chrysler Museum of Art. elizabethcatlett.net/.

Hayes, John R., ed. *The Genius of Arab Civilization: Source of Renaissance*. 3rd ed. New York: New York University Press, 1992.

Heffernan, Conor. "Katie Sandwina: The Strongest Woman in the World." Physical Culture Study. Sept. 7, 2017. physicalculturestudy.com/2017/09/07/katie-sandwina-the-strongest-woman-in-the-world/.

Herzog, Melanie Anne. *Elizabeth Catlett: An American Artist in Mexico*. Seattle: University of Washington Press, 2005.

Horwitz, Tony. "The Woman Who (Maybe) Struck Out Babe Ruth and Lou Gehrig." *Smithsonian*. July 2013. www.smithsonianmag.com/history/the-woman-who-maybe-struck-out-babe-ruth-and-lou-gehrig-4759182/.

Jones, David E. *Women Warriors: A History*. London: Brassey's Military Books, 1997.

Jones, Jae. "Lucy Hicks Anderson: Biologically Male, Lived as a Woman, and Jailed for Defrauding Government." Black Then, May 17, 2017. blackthen.com/lucy-hicks-anderson-biologically-male-lived-as-a-woman-and-jailed-for-defrauding-government/.

King, Oliver. "The Poll Tax Riot 25 Years Ago Was the Day I Woke Up Politically." *Guardian* (Manchester). March 31, 2015. www.theguardian.com/commentisfree/2015/mar/31/poll-tax-riots-25-years-ago-political-awakening-carnage-trafalgar-square.

Leonard, Kevin. "Anderson, Lucy Hicks [Tobias Lawson] (1886-1954)." African American History in the West. BlackPast.org. www.blackpast.org/aaw/anderson-lucy-hicks-1886-1954.

Lewis, Samella. *African American Art and Artists*, rev. ed. Berkeley: University of California Press, 2003.

Little, Benerson. *How History's Greatest Pirates Pillaged, Plundered, and Got Away with It: The Stories, Techniques, and Tactics of the Most Feared Sea Rovers from 1500–1800*. Beverly, MA: Fair Winds Press, 2010.

Lockard, Craig A. *Societies, Networks, and Transitions: A Global History* Vol. 1, *To 1500*. 3rd ed. Stamford, CT: Cengage Learning, 2015.

Lorde, Audre. *The Cancer Journals: Special Edition*. San Francisco, CA: Aunt Lute Books, 2006.

Mann, Susan. *Precious Records: Women in China's Long Eighteenth Century*. Stanford, CA: Stanford University Press, 1997.

Margaret Thatcher Foundation (website), 2017. www.margaretthatcher.org.

Marks, Tracy. "Artemisia: The Rape and the Trial." Artemisia, Renaissance Baroque Artist, 1999. www.webwinds.com/artemisia/trial.htm.

"Mary Frith Otherwise Moll Cutpurse: A Master-Thief and Ugly, Who Dressed Like a Man and Died in 1663." *The Newgate Calendar, or, Malefactors Bloody Register*. London, 1774.

Maynard, Olga. *Bird of Fire: The Story of Maria Tallchief*. New York: Dodd, Mead, 1961.

McMurry, Linda O. *To Keep the Waters Troubled: The Life of Ida B. Wells*. New York: Oxford University Press, 2000.

Middleton, Thomas, and Thomas Dekker. *The Roaring Girl, or Moll Cutpurse*. London, 1611.

Moore, Charles. *Margaret Thatcher: The Authorized Biography*. Vol. 2, *Everything She Wants*. London: Penguin, 2016.

Morris, Ivan. *The World of the Shining Prince: Court Life in Ancient Japan*. New York: Kodansha America, 1994.

Murasaki Shikibu. *The Diary of Lady Murasaki*. Translated by Richard Bowring. London: Penguin, 1996.

———. *The Tale of Genji* (abridged). Edited and translated by Royall Tyler. New York: Penguin, 2006.

Nelson, Cynthia. *Doria Shafik, Egyptian Feminist: A Woman Apart*. Cairo: American University in Cairo Press, 1996.

go Vinh Long and Nguyen Hoi Chan.
*Vietnamese Women in Society and
Revolution.* Vol. 1, *The French Colonial
Period.* Cambridge, MA: Vietnam Resource
Center, 1974.

oti, Iroegbu Chinaemerem. "Meet Fatima
al-Fihri: The Founder of the World's First
Library." Ventures Africa, Jan. 26, 2017.
vnt.rs/glh3u.

ennell, C. R., ed. *Bandits at Sea: A Pirates
Reader.* New York: New York University
Press, 2001.

eterson, Barbara Bennett, ed. *Notable Women
of China: Shang Dynasty to the Early
Twentieth Century.* Abingdon, UK:
Routledge, 2015.

izan, Christine de. *The Book of the City of
Ladies.* Translated by Rosalind
Brown-Grant. London: Penguin, 1999.

oggioli, Sylvia. "Long Seen as Victim, 17th
Century Italian Painter Emerges as Feminist
Icon." *All Things Considered.* NPR, Dec.
12, 2016.

agai, Aziza, and Jehane Ragai. Doria Shafik:
A Life Dedicated to Egyptian Women
(website), 2014. doria-shafik.com/.

chechter, Patricia A. *Ida B. Wells-Barnett and
American Reform, 1880–1930.* Chapel
Hill: University of North Carolina Press,
2001.

lide, Anthony. *Lois Weber: The Director Who
Lost Her Way in History.* Westport, CT:
Greenwood Press, 1996.

lide, Anthony. *The Silent Feminists: America's
First Women Directors.* Lanham, MD:
Scarecrow Press, 1996.

mitten, Richard. "The Godmother."

*Sun-Sentinel* (Fort Lauderdale). Feb. 19,
1989. articles.sun-sentinel.com/1989-02-19
/features/8901090931_1_liquor-store-store
-clerk-parking-lot.

Stamp, Shelley. *Lois Weber in Early
Hollywood.* Oakland: University of
California Press, 2015.

Stevenson, Jane. *Women Latin Poets:
Language, Gender, and Authority from
Antiquity to the Eighteenth Century.*
Oxford, UK: Oxford University Press, 2008.

Tallchief, Maria. *Maria Tallchief: America's
Prima Ballerina.* With Larry Kaplan. New
York: Holt, 1997.

Taylor, Keith Weller. *The Birth of Vietnam.*
Berkeley: University of California Press,
1991.

Thompson, Ben. "Ana Lezama de Urinza."
Badass of the Week. June 26, 2015.
badassoftheweek.com/index
.cgi?id=29009176046.

Todd, Jan. "Center Ring: Katie Sandwina and
the Construction of Celebrity." *Iron Game
History* 10, no. 1 (Nov. 2007): 4–13.

Todd, Janet, and Elizabeth Spearing, ed.
*Counterfeit Ladies: The Life and Death of
Mary Frith; The Case of Mary Carleton.*
New York: New York University Press,
1995.

Todd, Matthew. "Margaret Thatcher Was No
Poster Girl for Gay Rights." *Guardian*
(Manchester). April 10, 2013. www
.theguardian.com/commentisfree/2013
/apr/10/margaret-thatcher-poster-girl-gay
-rights.

Villarreal, Ryan. "Colombian Drug Lord
Griselda Blanco's Life of Violence Comes

Full Circle." *International Business Times.*
Sept. 4, 2012. www.ibtimes.com.

Watts, Edward J. *Hypatia: The Life and
Legend of an Ancient Philosopher.* New
York: Oxford University Press, 2017.

Weatherford, Jack. *The Secret History of the
Mongol Queens: How the Daughters of
Genghis Khan Rescued His Empire.* New
York: Broadway Paperbacks, 2015.

Weissberger, Barbara F., ed. *Queen Isabel I of
Castile: Power, Patronage, Persona.*
Woodbridge, UK: Tamesis, 2008.

Wells, Ida B. *Southern Horrors and Other
Writings: The Anti-Lynching Campaign of
Ida B. Wells, 1892–1900.* Edited by
Jacqueline Jones Royster. Boston: Bedford/
St. Martin's, 1996.

Wray, Lauren. "Legendary Bessie Stringfield
Motorcycle Queen." *Two Lanes Blog.*
Antique Archaeology. Aug. 3, 2015. www
.antiquearchaeology.com/blog/legendary
-bessie-stringfield-motorcycle-queen/.

Young, Greg. "Circus Activism: Barnum's
Female Stars Demand Right to Vote, Name
Baby Giraffe 'Miss Suffrage' at Madison
Square Garden." *The Bowery Boys* (blog).
March 30, 2012. www.boweryboyshistory
.com/2012/03/circus-activism-barnums
-female-stars.html.

Yule, Eleanor, director. *Michael Palin's Quest
for Artemisia.* Documentary film, 60 mins.
BBC4, 2015.

Yung-Lun Yüan. *History of the Pirates Who
Infested the China Sea from 1807 to 1810.*
Translated and edited by Karl Friedrich
Neumann. Cambridge, UK: Cambridge
University Press, 2011.

# ABOUT THE AUTHORS

ANITA SARKEESIAN is an award-winning media critic and the creator and executive director
of Feminist Frequency, an educational nonprofit that explores the representations of women in pop
ulture narratives. Best known as the creator and host of Feminist Frequency's highly influential series
Tropes vs Women in Video Games, Anita lectures at universities, conferences, and game development
studios around the world. Anita dreams of owning a life-size replica of Buffy's scythe.

EBONY ADAMS, PHD, is an author, activist, and former college educator whose work highlights
he lives and work of black women in the diaspora. She lives in Los Angeles with a steadily increasing
ollection of Doctor Who memorabilia. She writes widely on film criticism, social justice, and pop
ulture.